Our Own
Way

FINDING OUR OWN WAY

teachers exploring their assumptions

edited by

Judith M. Newman

Heinemann
Portsmouth, NH

Heinemann Educational Books, Inc.
70 Court Street
Portsmouth, NH 03801
Offices and agents throughout the world

Library of Congress Cataloging-in-Publication Data
Finding our own way : teachers exploring their assumptions / edited by
    Judith M. Newman.
        p. cm.
    Bibliography: p.1
    ISBN 0-435-08501-8
    1. Teaching.   2. Learning.   I. Newman, Judith, 1943-
LB1025.2.F5245   1990
371.1'02—dc20   89-15442
                                                                 CIP

Designed by Wladislaw Finne.
Printed in the United States of America.
10 9 8 7 6 5 4 3 2 1

Just Try

Chris Trussler

But I can't write a story!
Just try, I said.
How do you draw a cow?
Just try, I said.
I don't know how to read.
Just try, I said.
This is a "just try" school, said Joanna,
Mrs. Trussler said we just have to try.

Cows don't have six legs!
I tried, she said.
Isn't that book upside down?
I'm trying, he said.
I asked you to use a pencil.
I tried, she said.
What happened to our "just try" school?
Looks like *I'll* just have to try a bit harder.

Come and read with us.
I'll try, I said.
Come write with us.
I'll try, I said.
Talk and laugh and learn with us.
I'll try, I said.
But please be patient,
I'm learning too.

Contents

Marion Anderson has a varied teaching background. Presently a grade five teacher with the Halifax County–Bedford District School Board, she has taught children from kindergarten to junior high. She is interested in the role of teachers' intuition and school climate for nurturing students' learning.

Nancy Anthony is a resource teacher with the Halifax District School Board. She is exploring ways of helping students who have experienced failure in school to become successful, active learners.

Evelyn Bent is currently a junior–senior high school resource teacher with the Colchester–East Hants School Board. Her work with resource students has fostered her interest in the connection between students' reading and writing proficiency and their self-concept.

Beverly Boone is a junior high English teacher in Springdale, Newfoundland. Her recent focus has been on reading and writing across the curriculum.

Linda Christian, formerly a primary teacher, is now a program coordinator with the Avalon North Integrated School Board, Newfoundland. She is particularly interested in the collaborative nature of learning and the connection between reading and writing.

Christine Clark, previously a resource teacher, now teaches a grade two/three class with the Chester District School Board. She continues to explore language learning with her students through hands-on experiences in science and social studies.

Janice Clarke has been teaching elementary French in Dartmouth, Nova Scotia for the past three years. She also teaches English Language Arts for two grade three French Immersion Programme classes.

Linda Cook is a teaching vice-principal with the Halifax County–Bedford District School Board. She is interested in the development of children's reading and writing using a literature-based reading program.

Michael Coughlan, born and educated in Halifax, Nova Scotia, has taught grades seven through nine for thirteen years. He is actively implementing student-centered instruction in junior high. His particular focus involves the mainstreaming of learning disabled students.

Jan Gillin is a grade three teacher at the Halifax Grammar School. She is interested in exploring the use of drama in education.

Roberta Jones is a grade four teacher at the Convent of the Sacred Heart in Halifax, Nova Scotia. For some time, she has been intrigued by the language learning of preschoolers before the onset of formal education.

Florence Kanary is a junior high language arts teacher with the Halifax County–Bedford District School Board. She is involved in developing a literature-based reading/writing curriculum with her junior high classes.

pat kidd teaches junior high school students with the Halifax County–Bedford District School Board. Ever a student herself, she is particularly interested in students teaching teachers. Her students regularly conduct inservice sessions throughout the province of Nova Scotia.

Albert Layton has been both a secondary and elementary teacher for more than eighteen years. He is currently trying to create a whole language context with his elementary students. He is also exploring ways of using computers in his classroom.

Brian MacDonald has taught language arts at the junior high level for twelve years with the Cape Breton District School Board. His special interest is in curriculum design and implementation with a particular emphasis on the middle school years.

John S. Mayher is a Professor of English Education at New York University. Coauthor of *Learning to Write/Writing to Learn* (Boynton/Cook, 1983) and author of *Uncommon Sense: Theoretical Practice in Language Education* (Boynton/Cook, 1989), Dr. Mayher teaches and writes about critical professional inquiry. He is concerned about helping teachers become more responsible for their own teaching.

Judith M. Newman, a writer and education consultant, is a Professor of Education at Mount Saint Vincent University in Halifax, Nova Scotia. She teaches graduate classes in writing, reading, and the use of computers in the classroom. Her current research includes exploring ways of helping teachers become learners. She is author of *The Craft of Children's Writing* (Scholastic, 1984; distributed in the U.S. by Heinemann) and editor of *Whole Language: Theory in Use* (Heinemann, 1985).

Janet Ripley, an elementary school teacher in various Nova Scotia communities, is currently teaching with the Halifax County–Bedford District School Board.

Margot Shutt began her teaching career as a physical education specialist. She became interested in whole language as her own children began to learn to read. She now teaches a primary grade class with the Halifax District School Board.

Chris Trussler is on leave of absence from her position with the Halifax District School Board where she has taught since 1978. Chris is particularly interested in exploring her role as teacher/learner with beginning readers and writers.

Sumitra Unia is a grade five teacher with the Halifax District School Board. For several years she has been actively exploring the role of language in science learning.

Beth Valentine is a classroom teacher at Hawthorn Elementary School in Dartmouth, Nova Scotia. A teacher for fourteen years, she is extremely interested in involving children in their own learning.

Murray Wickwire is currently a teaching vice-principal with the Halifax County–Bedford District School Board. Murray is interested in writing as a vehicle for learning science and mathematics.

Fred Williams is a resource teacher, grades P–8, with the Northside–Victoria District School Board. His current major concern is finding ways of making reading and writing real in school situations.

Once upon a time, teachers and teacher educators could compla-
cently regard their task as being straightforward. There was expert
knowledge to be transmitted to the less knowledgeable: specific
bodies of content and skills to the young; another body of content
and techniques to preservice and inservice teachers. Various schools
of thought have considered different learning skills and teaching
techniques as essential, but the fundamental transmission framework
used for teaching has remained relatively unchallenged since the
demise of progressive education.

Recent perceptions of a crisis in education have given rise to two
general sorts of proposed solutions. The most common, and so
far the most influential, has not challenged the foundation of expert
transmission. Such "reforms" have led to attempts to control the
processes of schooling by mandating standardized testing for
children as young as five years old, have increased the use of
prestructured and preformulated curricula and teaching strategies,
and have lengthened the school day or the school year. Such "more
of the same" proposals have also included calls for more attention
to transmitting a common storehouse of knowledge—most recently
under the guise of cultural literacy—and have usually included a
special focus on the achievement of excellence in the name of
economic competitiveness. Seeking excellence from this perspective
seems to demand that special attention be paid to those students
in the top twenty percent of the population, since they are the only
ones deemed capable of such achievement. Although it is striking
that similar "reforms" have been proposed in all of the major
English-speaking democracies, neither the notion of education for
democracy nor the possibility of educational excellence for all has
been part of most calls for change.

Despite the attention of the powerful—politicians, the press, and even most educational "leaders"—to such proposals, another set of strong voices has emerged in language and literacy education. These voices from the classroom and from the teacher education community have begun to look afresh at the processes of learning and teaching and to raise important questions about the hows and whys of literacy education. We argue that the fundamental metaphors and theories of education must be reexamined, since more of the same will be no improvement if the underlying assumptions of traditional schooling are as deeply flawed as we believe they are.

Although this process of reexamination has been under way for more than twenty years, and indeed was prefigured in the work of John Dewey and others in the beginning of this century, it has yet to have much dramatic impact on the normal patterns of schooling. There are more tests and restrictive texts than ever before, more attempts to structure the classroom from outside its walls, and more controls placed on the autonomy of teachers and learners. One reason that alternative approaches fail to take hold is that they cannot be neatly prepackaged and do not fit comfortably within the traditional classroom format of expert transmission and numerical evaluation. Some bits and pieces of alternative ideas have begun to be adopted by some teachers and texts—most notably the "capital-*P*-for-Process" approach to the teaching of writing—but here, too, a progressive strategy has frequently been domesticated into a new version of what was formerly known as "outlining/ composing/proofreading/making a neat final copy."

Even more fundamentally, such ideas have been limited in their impact because they have more often raised questions than they have provided simple (and therefore packageable) answers. By doing so they have helped us recognize how complex the processes of learning and teaching really are, and the important role each particular classroom context plays in helping children grow and develop as language users. These questions and complexities have challenged both teachers and teacher educators to reimagine their roles and responsibilities in bringing about growth and change.

The metaphor of a journey of exploration, which provides the title of this volume, embodies the most fruitful kind of response by educators to these new challenges. It recognizes that since there are no maps or signs on the road to change, we must find our own way. It further emphasizes that while more experienced practitioners and theorists may provide us with a new vision of the road ahead, we are finally responsible for our own choices within our own teaching and learning contexts. We can learn with and from each other, but not in the sense of adopting wholesale a gimmick, recipe, or lesson plan—there are no tips here, no answers to the all too perennial question: what shall I do on Monday? What we can learn are the values of collaboration, of taking seriously the fundamental questions of learning and teaching, and most important of all, of the kinds of rewards that can come from risk taking in our teaching.

The teacher knowledge displayed in the essays collected here transcends what Stephen North (1987) has characterized as "lore" in his description of the kind of knowledge generated by practitioners.

For him the principal weaknesses of lore are the assumptions that what has "worked" for one teacher will "work" for another, and, most seriously, that because lore is deliberately eclectic and atheoretical, there is no way to ever eliminate anything from what he metaphorically characterizes as "the house of lore." By refusing the temptation to pretend that the experience of one teacher can be transferred unchanged to the classroom of another, these teacher-learners have implicitly challenged the first assumption of lore builders. They want us to learn with and from them, but only through enacting our own processes of finding our own way. And by implicitly and explicitly using theories of learning and teaching as the framework for reflecting on and evaluating their own practices, they have found a variety of means to measure the success of their actions. Doing so has enabled them to discard some of the most cherished aspects of their heritage of professional lore even though doing so has involved them in much more risky teaching.

For Judith Newman, who organized the course of study that brought these teacher-learners together, the risk comes from trying to enact her own principles of learning and teaching despite the conventional pattern of transmission teaching in tertiary education. Those of us who are struggling to go against the grain of our own schooling and the instructional patterns of our universities must constantly debate such questions as when to talk and when to keep silent, when to raise questions and when to let our students struggle on their own. The temptation to tell them what we know is always with us, however much we may understand that teacher telling does not lead to student learning unless the student has first formulated the question.

For the teacher-learners whose work makes up the bulk of this collection, the risks come from trying to reopen their most deeply held convictions about learning and teaching, to try to play a new and different role in their own classrooms, and to do so, often, without institutional comprehension and support. Nothing is easier than to stay with the tried and apparently true: that is the major appeal of practitioner lore. Nothing is harder than to put on new theoretical lenses that may help us see that the tried was not always true and that may also allow us to embark on a new journey without a well-planned route or a particularly clear map. One of the strengths of this collection is the individuality of these journeys and the courage each teacher-learner exhibits in confronting the inevitable challenges and obstacles on the new path.

Since each teacher-learner started the journey at a different place and is in charge of finding his or her own way, each report is necessarily idiosyncratic. Readers expecting to find The Word on teaching spelling or using literature to replace basal readers may be disappointed, but from my perspective that is not the way to read the book any more than it was the way it was written. What I have read it for are the voices of colleagues engaged in a mutual struggle to provide the best learning environments we can for the learners in our charge, whether they are in kindergarten or graduate school. By transacting with these stories of unfolding journeys, we can enrich and enlighten our own parallel, but necessarily individual, roads.

As I have often said, one of the major rewards of teaching as a profession is that no matter how good one gets at it, one can always find new routes to improvement. Like the teachers who tell their stories here, those of us who have embarked on this journey know that it will never end in the certainty of routine. As this year's experience becomes next year's, we can try to come closer to our own ideals while recognizing that even these are subject to change. This kind of open-ended ambiguity may not bring as much comfort as the good (bad?) old days of holding to the illusion that the road is premapped and the destination always clear, but if we understand that such certainty was an illusion—for our students if not for ourselves—we know we have no choice but to take these risks as we try to find our own way.

For me, the best response to this collection is not to take it as a set of notes on proven teaching practices or a collection of sure-fire lessons. It is not an addition to the house of lore, but it can provide us with a means to reflect on and critique our own practice. We should attempt to add our voices to those we find here. To become part of the conversation. To write our own chapters based on our experimentation and reflection, and to urge our students and colleagues to write theirs. To recognize that the greatest support we can expect from others is not the surety of adoptable answers, but the excitement and rewards of becoming part of a wider professional community that takes our journey seriously and recognizes the need for mutual respect along the way.

John S. Mayher
New York University

Reference

North, Stephen M. 1987. *The Making of Knowledge in Composition*. Portsmouth, NH: Boynton/Cook.

Not long ago, I conducted a daylong inservice with a group of teachers and administrators. We began the workshop by listing all the writing that we ourselves had done during the previous week and making note of its purposes and audiences. We followed that activity by making a similar list of our students' writing. Comparisons between the two lists made evident some important questions about why and for whom our students write. It was apparent, despite considerable attention over the last few years to what is being called a "process approach to writing," that much student writing is still being done primarily for grading purposes.

I invited the teachers and administrators to explore other purposes for writing, other ways of using writing for learning. We freewrote. We played with written responses to some stories. We made brief notes in preparation for group discussion, then wrote gist statements to summarize what was said. We prepared a collaborative synopsis of the group deliberations and engaged in written conversations about the issues. We did a lot of writing and we shared much of it. We ended the workshop by listing the diverse purposes and audiences for the writing we'd done, and the teachers identified many different ways they could use these various kinds of writing in their classrooms. Nevertheless, at the end of the session a number of participants were angry because they felt they'd received nothing practical. Their reaction forced me to think about whole language and about how to help teachers understand the intricacies of implementing this theoretical perspective.

What, in fact, is whole language? Whole language is not a ready-made commercial instructional package, notwithstanding the now numerous basal reading programs blazoned with the slogan. Whole language is a philosophical stance incorporating the theoretical insights from recent research in such diverse disciplines as socio-

1

psycholinguistics, linguistics, sociology, anthropology, philosophy, child development, curriculum, composition, literary theory, semiotics, and other fields of study. As with all such theoretical arguments, the practical ramifications are open to interpretation. Teachers have to explore the implementation of these research insights in their own classrooms based on what they've discovered about the needs, interests, instructional history, and proficiency of individual students.

There are some guiding principles:

- Language learning is a social activity; it occurs best when there is discussion and a sharing of knowledge and ideas between teachers and students and among students.
- Language learning is a global enterprise; the processes involved in writing, reading, talking, and listening are closely interwoven.
- Learning involves risk, since mistakes are expected to occur in any genuine learning situation. Consequently, learners have to be able to exercise some control over their own learning. They have to have some input into curricular decision making.

These principles provide a framework for creating a learning context that offers continous demonstrations about how meaning is constructed by an interpretive community, about how reading and writing are collaborative activities, and about how oral and written language are tools for learning. These principles allow teachers and students to be learners together. These principles make teaching a theoretical endeavor.

Although keeping journals, using Big Books, reading and discussing children's literature, setting up reading and writing centers, initiating authoring circles, arranging furniture in specific configurations, and establishing a flexible schedule are all part of establishing a whole language environment, these specific implementations don't necessarily depict an open, learner-directed classroom. Creating a whole language learning environment demands more. It requires that we engage in an ongoing reexamination of our beliefs and assumptions about learning and teaching, and about using language to learn about the world. It requires that teachers become open to learning both with and from our students.

The real problem with becoming a whole language teacher has to do with the gulf between what we say we believe and what our actions convey to students about what really counts. The fact is, all too often our instructional practices contradict the beliefs we espouse. We think we're allowing students greater responsibility and freedom with their reading and/or writing—only to discover that many of our instructional and grading practices still really leave control of the learning in our hands.

The process of changing from a traditional transmission way of teaching to creating an open, learner-directed environment is complex. There are no shortcuts, no fifty "nifty tips." It isn't enough just to buy different books or prepare new activities. A profound philosophical shift is necessary—a shift supported by constantly updating our theoretical understanding, by learning more about what is involved in how language is learned and used, and by always questioning our instructional objectives and practices.

There is a growing body of resources for helping teachers develop a whole language-based classroom. Many books and articles have been written about various aspects of literacy development. They describe a variety of instructional situations to show others the strengths of children's learning when they are emersed in a learner-centered environment. Many teachers attempt to replicate blindly the instructional recipes offered. Other teachers react defensively to these descriptions. The classroom activities, the context they present, imply a coherence few teachers have experienced in their own teaching. They are sometimes overwhelmed by the contradictions between these classrooms and their own. As one teacher put it, these writings make her feel that

a whole language classroom is a place for saints only—a place where wonderful teachers do incredibly wonderful things for magnificent reasons and the results are always miraculous. I'm a regular teacher trying to do a good job. I care about my kids, but there isn't a hope that I could ever be that good, that wonderful. It's discouraging.

This from a competent teacher, actively trying to change what's occurring in her classroom. The tidy descriptions of what should be happening with her students is unlike anything she's experienced. There have been hitches with almost everything she's attempted. Even so, she's still committed to exploring a more student-centered learning environment. She wants and needs support that acknowledges changing as a messy and uncertain venture. The aim of this book is to examine some of that mess and uncertainty.

The articles that form the body of this collection were written by teachers, all of whom have participated in my "Writing and Computers" graduate course. Eighteen of the articles were written by the Winter 1987–88 class in response to my invitation that we try writing for other teachers. The other five articles were written during the previous two years.

"Writing and Computers" is a year-long course on writing and writing instruction. In it, we look at conflicting theories of writing as well as the research on writing development. We pay particular attention to reading/writing relationships. We also explore various writing strategies by becoming writers ourselves. Almost all of our writing is done on computer, and for many in the group that means learning to use one. However, while computers are important for allowing us to accomplish our ends, writing and writing instruction remain the focus of our exploration.

I have been offering this course since 1983. Each year, the graduate students and I grope our way toward a new understanding of writing and reading, learning and teaching. By becoming a writing community, the teachers and I have learned many useful things about writing and writing instruction. We have, for example, discovered how writing can change the writer. We've experienced the power of reading like writers and seen how the sharing of one another's efforts has let us find solutions to our writing dilemmas.

We've learned that writers needn't be left on their own to face the decision making involved in working out a piece. We've also learned that to be effective teachers of writing, we must be writers too. By experiencing the vulnerability of being writers, we have discovered many kinds of support that can help students develop their writing proficiency. In our struggles with conflicting views about writing and reading, the teachers and I have had important insights about learning and teaching. This collection of articles reflects the substance of many of our class discussions.

Writing isn't the only vehicle for helping us examine the complex issues of literacy instruction. We have read widely. The numerous books and articles that we read and discussed (see Selected Readings) have also raised important questions and issues that encouraged the teachers to reflect on their beliefs and assumptions. Their reading made them members of a broader interpretive community, one that engages in critical examination of learning and teaching. The arguments and theoretical discussions that they encountered greatly affected how the teachers thought about themselves, their writing, and their teaching. Although in writing about their insights and experiences the teachers cite few references, without that contact with the larger research community these articles couldn't have been written. It was their reading that helped these teachers elect to join the professional conversation.

Finding Our Own Way is about change. Not change in the abstract, or change for the sake of change, but change in a particular direction: toward a more flexible, interpretive view of the world and of learning and teaching. It's not a "how to" book. It offers few tips. Instead, the teachers and I have written to share our questions, some of the conflicts we've experienced, and a sense of changing beliefs which becoming a learner-directed teacher entails.

In this collection of articles is the realization that teaching is a learning enterprise and that teachers are learners too. For many of these teachers, it was both a surprise and a delight to discover that their students could teach them a great deal. However, this insight raised many difficult questions about being a teacher. Our writing has helped us realize that we have to see what our students are showing us, not just listen to what the books and experts have to say. It has made us aware that we must become our own experts. For some of the teachers, discovering that no one can tell them exactly what they should be doing and how they should do it has been uncomfortable. Others have found the discovery liberating. It has allowed them to explore new avenues without feeling guilty.

We have learned that there is no one right way, no one right answer to any question about teaching. Every question can, and perhaps should, be answered with, "It depends." It depends on what has gone before, on what the students seem to know, on the strategies they have at their disposal at the moment, on how ready they seem to be to forge ahead, on how far we think we can push the conventional expectations of the wider context of the school and community.

Every one of the teachers who has contributed to this collection of articles has begun an important journey. People started at different places, took different paths, and had different experiences along the way. As their teacher and guide, I watched them all confront major obstacles and, in surmounting them, forge ahead. Everyone has taken risks. Although some have journeyed farther than others, they've all allowed themselves to be vulnerable in some significant way. As was to be expected, their progress as writers, as learners, and as teachers has been uneven. Nevertheless, everyone has grown. For readers uncomfortable with the evident unevenness and inconsistencies in this collection of articles, I would ask you to consider using these teachers' stories to help you reflect on your own theoretical beliefs and practices. Use your disagreements with what they've had to say to examine your own pedagogical assumptions and think about what you would do in their situations.

An important concern for me is what happens to these teachers when they leave the intense and supportive interpretive community that the class has provided. Will they be able to continue their quest? Will they seek out new guides from the research literature and professional associations? Will they engage colleagues in their conversation? Will they continue learning with and from their students?

The last twenty years has seen considerable educational change, particularly in the realm of language instruction. It hasn't been a sweeping change, not a whirlwind irrevocably altering the educational landscape. The change has been more subtle, more gradual, with individual teachers like those who have written here having begun to alter their teaching in very substantial ways. Their move away from a traditional transmission focus toward a more open, learner-directed classroom has often been a difficult and sometimes lonely quest. In writing these articles, we are trying to provide some support and encouragement for others attempting the same journey.

Finding Our
Own Way
Judith M. Newman

Recently, a teacher in one of my graduate classes remained behind to ask a question. "If I'm writing when my students are," she wanted to know, "when do I find time to talk with them about their own writing?" A good question, I thought, and I was about to tell her what I would do. But I caught myself. I sensed her hidden question: "Am I doing this right?" Had I given her a direct answer, I wouldn't have helped her think through the problem herself. Had I given her tips, had I told her what I might do in her situation, the next time she had questions she might go looking for authoritative answers and not take the time to reflect on her own about the choices she has and what each might convey to her students.

So I answered by asking a question. "What reasons do you have for writing when they do?" She explained how she wanted her third graders to see how she thought writing was an important activity, important enough for her to be doing it too. She also wanted an opportunity to demonstrate some of the mess of writing. By writing when her students were, she could share some of her writing strategies. "How often during the day are the children writing?" I asked her. "What different kinds of writing are they doing?" "Do you have to be writing with them every time they write?" As I continued probing, the teacher began to see how she could fulfill her various objectives by engaging in a number of different activities while her students were busy writing. She realized there was no one thing she *should* be doing every time her students wrote.

I relate this incident because it demonstrates clearly the kind of decisions I, like every teacher, face constantly. Do I answer a particular question directly or would it be more useful to mention something to read that might clarify the matter? Do I ask a question, as I did in this case, or suggest it might be helpful to discuss the

7

concern with a couple of others in the class? Or do I take the question and use it later as the basis for an experience for the whole group so everyone can think about the problem? I don't have a long time to deliberate about what course of action to take—I have to make a decision and respond immediately; that's what conversations are like.

My choice of strategy in such a situation is determined by a number of factors: my assumptions about what teaching means, what I sense might be useful for an individual or group of students at that particular moment, and my awareness of my own learning/teaching strategies. I am aware of some (although by no means all) of the beliefs that currently guide my instructional decision making. I haven't always held these beliefs; they've been evolving for more than twenty years.

My current thinking about teaching is the result of a long journey. When I began as a high school science teacher, I assumed, as did most of my fellow teachers, that my students knew very little and my responsibility was to dispense the facts, to assign exercises and drills for them to practice the stuff, and to correct and grade their assignments. Like many other teachers, I was reasonably comfortable with the idea of teaching as transmitting information. But the formal studying I have done, my continuing engagement with the research literature, the ongoing conversation with other teachers, discussions with friends and colleagues, and, most important, my involvement with students (children as well as adults), have helped me grow and change as a teacher.

One of my current beliefs is that learning is a collaborative enterprise. People don't learn in isolation. They learn by being members of a learning community. While we each construct an individual interpretation of a particular situation, our understanding is shaped by contact with other people's perceptions of what's gone on. Our interpretation will hold until we become aware of a discrepancy either through some direct personal experience or from something we've heard or read elsewhere and discuss it anew.

Another belief is that we don't learn about speaking and listening, writing and reading, by having to deal with them as separate entities. I've become convinced that these language systems are intimately interconnected. I've discovered the impact that reading can have on writing and that writing can have on reading. I have had, for example, the experience of struggling to write about a particular idea and finding a solution in something I happen to be reading, or I have recognized an author's stylistic or organizational tactic I've recently used myself. Furthermore, I have learned about writing when talking to other writers about their writing, and listening to what they have to say about mine. My experience isn't unique. Many people I've talked to about the interconnectedness of the various aspects of language describe similar experiences.

I'm also convinced of the crucial role risk taking plays in learning. Mistakes afford us an opportunity to enlarge or reshape our interpretation of our experiences. In effect, what we know is a reflection of the various problems we've had to identify and sort out.

Learning involves exploring unknown territory, but learners aren't likely to reach beyond themselves if they expect to be embarrassed or are made to feel stupid. In such circumstances people tend to be cautious. If, however, they trust that their efforts will be accepted and they'll be helped to refine what they're trying to accomplish, learners are far more willing to attempt the difficult and unfamiliar. In order for learners to be willing to risk being vulnerable they have to have some control over what is being done, how it is being done, and why it's being done. The best way to exercise control is to be involved in making decisions. Choice, then, becomes an essential element in any risk-taking situation.

In short, learning—language learning in particular—is a collaborative, global, risky business. Learners play a crucial role in creating knowledge and language for themselves. They must constantly experiment, try things out, and make adjustments as they see how a particular learning endeavor is faring.

To maximize students' learning potential, I believe teachers have to become learners as well. There are two aspects to becoming a learning teacher. First, there has to be a shift in role. Instead of transmitting information, we must discover how to invite students into the learning arena, how to create situations in which students see other people doing what they can begin to imagine doing themselves, how to sustain their participation in the group enterprise, how to keep conversations going, and how to respond to what they are trying to do. Second, through students' participation we learn about their interests, their strategies, and their difficulties. By following where students lead, we allow them to show us new directions to pursue, and we discover their potential for learning. Every teaching encounter becomes an opportunity for us to discover new things both about learning and about how to assist individual learners.

Every teacher wonders, "Am I doing this right?" The answer must come primarily from our engagement with our students—not from the assurances and suggestions of outside experts. When we shift from teacher-driven learning to learner-directed teaching we become learners too.

Becoming a learner-directed teacher involves being receptive to the unexpected. Like our students, we have to be willing to take risks. That doesn't mean abandoning objectives or working without a curricular framework. It means offering students an invitation to explore in some specific direction and then following closely behind. To allow learners to direct me, I have to be prepared to learn from them.

In the Classroom

Let me show how I try to implement my instructional beliefs by describing a particular learning/teaching experience I had with an Australian first-grade class.

Inta Gollasch, the teacher, had invited me to spend a morning in her classroom. She had said I was welcome to take charge of the classroom for the three hours I would be there. I was free to engage the children in whatever learning experiences I thought they might enjoy.

Before the children arrived I'd browsed around the room. I'd examined books in the library corner. I'd sampled some of the children's writing. I was trying to develop a feeling for who these children were, what interested them, and how fluently they could write and read. I didn't have a specific instructional plan, that is, I hadn't spent the previous evening preparing an elaborate lesson. I was interested more in finding a point of departure from my initial engagement with the children. I was on the alert for any invitation they might offer me.

When the children appeared, Inta introduced me and asked me to share something about Canada with them. The first thing that came to mind was one of my favorite Canadian children's stories by Sue Ann Alderson (1974). I didn't have the book with me, but I've read it often enough that I almost know it by heart, so I launched into the wrongdoings of Bonnie McSmithers.

The children were sitting on the floor in front of me listening with intense absorption to the litany of Bonnie's misdemeanors: getting covered with mud while playing outdoors, "cleaning" the bathroom with toothpaste and shampoo, cutting the buttons from her jacket, and so on. Each time I recited the refrain "Bonnie McSmithers, you're driving me dithers and blithery, blathery out of my mind....", the chorus swelled as more and more children joined in.

When I finished telling the story, I invited the children to share incidents of their own. "What sorts of things have you done that have made your parents say 'you're driving me dithers?' " I asked them. There was no hesitation. One child after another described some occasion when he or she had inadvertently been naughty. Everyone had a story to tell.

As the children were recounting their misdeeds, I was thinking about how to bring reading and writing into the experience. It occurred to me they might enjoy having a copy of *Bonnie McSmithers, You're Driving Me Dithers* to read. We could create one together. "Would you like to try writing your stories out?" I asked them. "Then we could put them together as a book." Most of the children were interested in having a go at it. Within moments they were engrossed in recording some personal incident for the class publication. Those who weren't, asked if they might work on other writing or read in the reading center. That was fine both with Inta and with me.

Inta and I moved around the room, offering whatever help seemed necessary. One child looked hesitant—"Tell me about a time when you did something that made your mum or dad angry." Another asked about the spelling of a word—"Have a try, see how you think it goes." Someone else showed me what she'd written so far—"That is definitely a 'Bonnie story,' " I said. "What was going on before you knocked the ashes from the fireplace all over the new carpet?"

My initial intention had been simply to compile the children's writing. But when I saw that they were writing on various sizes of paper, I thought it would be fun to make a class Big Book, incorporating their incidents into a single Bonnie story. Once the children seemed to have their writing under control, I took some large paper and began writing out our version of *Bonnie McSmithers*.

Bonnie McSmithers was a little girl with brown hair, brown eyes, and freckles all over her nose. She tried hard to be good, but she always seemed to get into trouble. And then her mother would say:
Bonnie McSmithers, you're driving me dithers
And blithery, blathery out of my mind.
How do you think of such things to do?
What am I going to do with you?
Now, be a good girl
And behave yourself.

One day . . .

I was now ready for some incidents. As children finished what they were writing, they brought the incidents to me to be included in the Big Book. There were stories about playing in the leaves and falling in the mud. There were stories about cutting sister's hair, taking a bath and then cleaning the shower door with toothpaste, and putting eggs in the microwave. I had the children help me recast their incidents, some true, some fictitious, as "Bonnie" stories as I printed them out on the large paper. Between each tale of disaster I inserted the refrain, "Bonnie McSmithers, you're driving me dithers. . . ."

Having written out eight mishaps, however, I shifted unexpectedly from being a teacher to being a writer. I suddenly realized that stories have a point. Our story needed an ending! I couldn't just compile the children's tales. At that moment I recognized I had to do more than act as scribe. There had to be some way of making a coherent whole out of these various incidents. (The original ends with Bonnie finally becoming angry with her mother for continually nagging her and retorting, "Mommy McSmithers, you're driving me dithers. . . ." Bonnie resolves the dilemma by asking her mother to play with her, and her mother discovers that Bonnie gets into less mischief when they do things together.) I discussed the problem with the children. "How can we finish our story?" A number of children thought Bonnie's mother should threaten to punish her if she wasn't more careful. I agreed that was one way to end it. "Are there others?" I asked.

A couple of children and I explored possible endings during recess. One child proposed Bonnie's dad do something silly, which would let Bonnie chastise him. "What could he do?" We considered a number of options and finally settled on having Bonnie's dad knock over a can of paint and spill some on the furniture while redecorating the living room. I wrote out our ending and then read the book to the class. Yet the story still seemed unfinished to me. Yes, parents can get into trouble, but we needed to illustrate this in a way that would connect back to Bonnie and her experiences.

As we discussed the point of our story, a child commented, "Well, everybody has accidents sometimes." Yes, I thought, that's it.

Bonnie's dad could comment that everyone does things they don't mean to do and get into trouble because of it. That would acknowledge Bonnie doesn't do naughty things intentionally; instead, much of her mischief results from not thinking ahead. "How can we write that?" I asked. I took a piece of paper and in front of the children transcribed their ideas. I wrote something, read it aloud, and scratched things out a couple of times before we settled on

> "Well," said Bonnie's Dad, "everyone has accidents sometimes."
> "Yes," replied Bonnie, "they do!"
> After that, whenever Bonnie did something that got her into trouble, her parents didn't say
> "Bonnie McSmithers, you're driving me dithers
> And blithery, blathery out of my mind."
> They said instead, "Oh, dear! I guess, everyone can have accidents, can't they?"

After I copied out our ending to the story, I realized we didn't have a title. I asked the children for suggestions. They decided on *Bonnie McSmithers, You're Driving Me Dithers*!" I created a title page, arranged the pages, and stapled them. Then we read the whole story aloud together.

The Learning Enterprise

Trying to be both a learner-directed and a learning teacher is a complicated undertaking. It involves opting for risk, not security. While I had a general sense of what I might do with these children whom I'd never met before, I had no carefully detailed lesson plan. I hadn't, for example, worked out precise objectives and activities before meeting them. I did know I wanted to capitalize on the children's interests and, based on what they showed me they could do, I intended to explore writing and reading a bit further with them. That meant I had to be prepared to go in whatever directions the children offered me. To be able to follow the children's lead I had to know quite a bit about how reading and writing are learned. I also had to have some sense of how to extend an open invitation so each of the children could find a way into the experience for him or herself. I had to know how to make them feel comfortable enough to be willing to take some risks. I had to be ready for openings to collaborate with the children as well as to encourage them to collaborate with one another.

The collaborative nature of our enterprise was obvious in a variety of ways. The sharing began with the children relating tales of dreadful behavior prompted by my relating Bonnie's misdeeds. Many of the children elected to write about similar incidents. Few of those writing an incident were at a loss for something to write about; lots of stories were readily available. What was interesting was how the children didn't use the exact Bonnie incidents I'd told, but adapted them in some personal way. Like Bonnie McSmithers's mishaps, the children's incidents were all about inadvertent misbehavior. No one told of purposely being bad or mean; they had all understood the point of the story: if we don't consider consequences we may find ourselves in trouble.

The children collaborated with each other and with me in still other ways. They chatted about their writing and helped one another out with ideas and functional spelling of unfamiliar words. They helped me with suggestions for incorporating specific children's incidents. They helped me work out an ending to make the point of what we were writing explicit. Our final copy of the book was as much theirs as it was mine (and Sue Ann Alderson's). The children were also helping one another as readers. Our choral reading of the book at various points in its production helped those children who were not yet independent readers figure out what those particular marks on the page were all about.

This particular brief learning experience incorporated many aspects of language: it involved talking, listening, writing, reading, and much storytelling. It arose from a conversation that provided an opening for me to slip into storytelling. Had I had the book at hand, I might actually have read it, but the telling of it was, I'm sure, equally valuable. It offered the children a narrative with which to engage and to connect to their own experiences. The predictability of the refrain drew in even the most insecure children. My invitation to recount some similar experiences gave them a chance to share their own misdeeds. Their telling served as a bridge to writing.

While the children were writing, there was a great deal of talking and giggling going on as they discussed and read their particular incidents with one another. Most couldn't wait for Inta or me to come around; they sought us out to chuckle about the naughty behavior they had decided to describe.

As I began transcribing the story, children wanted to read what I was writing. At several points I stopped and had them read with me what I'd written. We talked about the evolving story, about their incidents and how to incorporate them into the whole. It was impossible to distinguish between talk about the writing and the actual writing itself as they helped me compose sentences and decide upon wording.

Both choice and risk were fundamental aspects of this learning situation. Within the global invitation—let's try writing our own version of *Bonnie McSmithers*—there was ample room for choice. The children were free to choose to participate or to select some other activity. If they chose to write, they decided what to write about and how to write it. Then they had control over how I transcribed their particular contribution and added it to the evolving book.

A consequence of inviting the children to take charge was their willingness to take risks. I was trying to establish a "just try" context—one in which the children would be willing to extend themselves. I wanted them to feel comfortable writing unfamiliar words, exploring new ideas. For that reason I chose to "just try" myself. It seemed like a good opportunity to let them see how others deal with the kinds of decisions writers have to make. Because I didn't have the book planned in advance, the children saw me write something, change my mind, cross out, rewrite, and recopy as I went along. They could see how writing, at least for me, is a messy business involving false starts and much reworking and rethinking.

This *Bonnie McSmithers* experience was but one small addition to the complex language learning environment for the first-grade children in that class. The activity itself involved the majority of the class for just under an hour; while I continued working on the book, the children went on with other activities. During the morning they read other books on their own, in pairs, in small groups, with Inta, their teacher, with a fifth-grade partner, and with me. Some wrote in their daily journals. Others wrote notes to one another and to their teacher. Some of the less proficient children had an opportunity to compose at the computer with the help of their fifth-grade partners. When I needed help with *Bonnie McSmithers*, I was able to turn to the nearest small group for input without seriously interrupting what they were doing.

And all the while Inta and I were busy teaching—we were creating invitations to explore written language, suggesting resources to individual children, responding to questions about spelling and text organization, commenting about passages being read, sustaining the continuous conversation about written language by being a part of it.

The *Bonnie McSmithers* experience didn't end when I left the classroom at noon on Friday. On Monday, one child explored a fictional account of Bonnie's birthday in her daily journal, drawing upon some recent reading experiences to embellish her writing ("Bonnie dressed very daintily"). Several other children continued working on their "Bonnie" incidents. They said they wanted to compile a second version of the book because their incidents hadn't been included in the first. To support them, Inta read *Bonnie* aloud with the children to make the text structure available once again. Without any formal discussion, a number of children shifted from writing personal narrative ("When I was ...") to fiction ("she did ... and when her mother saw her ..."). The previous compiling of their individual stories had made them aware of the shift in genre. On their own, they changed from first to third person.

While I was creating our *Bonnie* book I intentionally slipped in a couple of subtle demonstrations to see what might happen. In a few places I emphasized some of the words by altering the way I printed them—I wrote the word *horrible* in large open letters, for example. I used underlining for emphasis. I also made a point of using a variety of punctuation. I put in some large exclamation marks and preceded each appearance of the refrain with a colon ("and then her mother would say:").

Both of these demonstrations had an impact. One child used large open letters for emphasis in her daily journal later that morning. On Monday, another used the colon in exactly the same way I had—("and then her mother would say:").

Yes, *Bonnie McSmithers* proved a useful learning experience for the children. They had a great time talking and writing about getting into mischief and incidentally learned a little more about reading and writing.

But I was learning too. I learned something new about story

writing. My initial plan had been simply to create a Big Book by compiling the children's stories. The fact that we required a focused ending didn't occur to me until I had transcribed a number of misdeeds. It was at that moment I became actively involved in the writing myself; I realized we needed some way to connect these separate incidents. My appreciation for authors of children's stories grew immeasurably as I discovered firsthand just how difficult creating an appropriate ending can be.

I also learned once more about the importance of trusting children's innate interest in learning to help me make new connections for myself. It was the children's incidents and our subsequent discussion of what they were all about that let me find a way to pull the book together. They were able to help me work out a solution to what had become a personal writing problem.

And I saw, once again, the need for giving children room to make their own connections. By observing the children as they engaged in the various writing and reading activities, I was able to determine just what sort of assistance I might offer. The children showed me which of them were ready to engage with particular aspects of reading and writing. I was taking my lead from them.

Changing

My journey from being a traditional transmission teacher to one who believes in knowledge as something learners must create for themselves has been a lengthy one. I've come a long way from my beginnings as a transmission high school science teacher. Each step of the way I've had to face many assumptions about learning and teaching, and I've had to change often. My experiences with disturbed adolescents and special education students made me question prevailing notions about what constitutes appropriate curriculum and what we should be teaching students. My many years as a math tutor helped me shift my focus from teacher-driven learning to learner-directed teaching. Teaching teachers has continued to force me to grow. And my journey hasn't ended. Each new group of teachers presents me with important challenges. Every class affords me new learning opportunities.

What about others wanting to become learning teachers? Clearly such a theoretical shift isn't easy to accomplish. Change has to come from within. To adopt a learning stance, people have to become aware of what they believe about learning and teaching and to consider how those beliefs affect their instructional decisions and practices. They have to be prepared to confront contradictions. That means taking a close look at their own teaching. Unfortunately, teachers generally do not work at making sense of their own classrooms. They often take someone else's experiences and then attempt to impose that secondhand sense on what they're doing. As David Dillon (1988) points out, "This tactic can cut them off from their experience in their own classrooms more than it can give them a purchase on it" (p. 269).

Teachers' dependence on the expertise of others isn't difficult to understand. From our own schooling experiences to inservice for professional development, we are faced with a transmission view of learning and teaching. At every turn we are being told how and what we should teach. Rarely are we encouraged and helped to think through a situation for ourselves. Instead, districtwide adoption of published programs in all areas of the curriculum conveys the not-so-subtle message that we can't be trusted to make sensitive, intelligent instructional decisions, that people at a distant remove from the classroom are in a better position to know how to teach children with whom they will never have contact. Furthermore, as Stephen North (1987) discusses, there has been a concerted effort on the part of scholars and researchers, makers of alternate brands of knowledge, to devalue what we have come to know from our own experience. The credibility of knowledge created as a result of the act of teaching and its power in regard to other kinds of knowledge has steadily diminished. So it shouldn't be surprising that most teachers have come to rely on other people's experience and expertise.

The people to whom teachers turn for answers are, as Dillon discusses, most frequently the "experts"—district consultants, program developers, published scholars and researchers, university professors. Rarely are they fellow practitioners. The problem with teachers' dependence on the experts' knowledge is that the experts seldom make their assumptions about learning and teaching explicit. And seldom do they have any personal teaching experience with the particular learners in question. Even the suggestions of other classroom teachers are of minimal use because other people's solutions can never be adopted blindly.

There are a number of reasons why other people's solutions have limited value, of course. The decisions that need to be made in each instructional situation are affected by what we know and believe. Furthermore, our own instructional and teaching histories affect how we perceive the particular instructional problem we're trying to solve. The constraints set up by the school community affect our teaching decisions. And the expectations of the community at large, of our students' parents, impact on our instructional implementation. Not only is each teacher unique, but every student is different also: each has had a different instructional history and different home experience. So while we can learn from what others have done or are trying to do, we still have to create each teaching situation anew for ourselves.

How can we come to value our own experience and trust our own judgments? The answer is simple. We need to see teaching as a learning endeavor. How can we become learners in our own classrooms? We become learning teachers when we begin to reflect on what we believe and why we're doing what we're doing. Our daily involvement with students presents many opportunities for thinking about our beliefs and practices as teachers. In a social learning context, students are continually commenting on procedures, making connections, questioning decisions, asking for information. These questions and comments have potential for letting us learn both about ourselves and our students.

Significant learning moments don't only occur in the classroom.

Something we read may force us to take stock. An overheard comment can make us wonder. Noticing how someone else is doing something we've always taken for granted, or suddenly seeing our own learning strategies with new eyes, can help us learn more about being teachers. Whatever the source, potential critical moments are everywhere, and they offer important opportunities for becoming reflective practitioners. First, however, we have to become aware of those moments and the possibilities they offer.

Critical Incidents

The following story told by Sue Curtis, an Australian teacher, tells of such an instance. Sue had been grocery shopping when she became aware of a young boy apparently on the verge of panic, rushing up and down the aisles of the supermarket.

I stopped him and asked if he was lost. He said he was. I took his hand and told him I was good at finding moms.
"Tell me when you see your mom," I said to him. Together we walked up and down the aisles. However, after about ten minutes we still hadn't found his mother. So I took the child to a nearby checkout counter, stood him on it, and then asked him to take a look around and tell me when he could see his mother. No response. I finally asked, "Can't you see your mother?"
"No," the child replied, "I can only see my Daddy."

For Sue Curtis this is a story about asking wrong questions. The incident helped her think about the numerous occasions in her classroom when she asked wrong questions of her students. For me, this story goes further; it highlights the assumptions upon which our wrong questions are based. In Sue's case, this particular wrong question was prompted by her assuming that mothers, not fathers, do the family grocery shopping. Similarly, in the classroom many of our wrong questions result from inappropriate assumptions. Sometimes we're fortunate and our students respond in such a way that we're helped to examine some of those assumptions. Often, however, we remain unaware of the discrepancy between what *we* think is occurring and our students' perceptions of what is happening.

Sue Curtis's story is an example of what I call a critical incident. Critical incidents are those occurrences that let us see with new eyes some aspect of what we do. They make us aware of the beliefs and assumptions that underlie our instructional practices. The incident made Sue examine herself and her teaching. Although it didn't occur in the classroom, she saw a connection between what had happened with that child in the supermarket and what often happens with her students. It made her more aware of the questions she was asking them.

Although we aren't generally aware of it, everything we do in the classroom is founded on a set of beliefs about learning and teaching, about knowledge, and about what counts as legitimate reading and writing. We operate on the basis of what Chris Argyris

(1976) calls our action theory. What's interesting is that this action theory is rarely explicitly worked out. It comes from our own experiences as readers and writers and from the kind of instruction we experienced in school ourselves. In effect, our beliefs about learning and teaching are largely tacit. We operate a good deal of the time from an intuitive sense of what is going on without actively reflecting on what our intentions might be and what our actions could be saying to students. Unfortunately, this means that much of the time we have little contact with what students are actually learning from our instructional activities. In order to understand what students are learning, we first have to make our theories explicit and open to scrutiny.

Exploring critical incidents has proven to be a useful way of learning more about my own teaching and for helping other teachers examine their instructional assumptions. I started using critical incidents with my graduate students, all of whom are teachers, as a way of finding out more about our current beliefs and about the assumptions underlying what we are doing in our classrooms. We began collecting and sharing stories, which contributed to our understanding about language and learning and about our role as teachers. Sometimes the incidents confirmed what we believed; more often, however, we were forced to reappraise our assumptions. What these critical incidents frequently revealed was a surprising gap between what we said we believed about learning and teaching (our espoused beliefs) and what our actions were conveying.

As we collected incidents and categorized them I noticed that those which help us change as teachers aren't big events—they're the small everyday ongoing occurrences. Our learning opportunities come from comments made in passing, from a statement overheard, from something a student might write in a journal, from something we might read either because it confirms our experiences or because we disagree and have to consider what we believe instead or because it opens possibilities we haven't thought about before. I also realized the learning remains hidden unless we have some reason for making it explicit. Writing the stories down became an important part of uncovering our assumptions. It forced us to explain these situations to ourselves.

Engaging in this kind of analysis wasn't easy. We needed to ask one another such questions as

- why is this incident memorable?
- what do I learn from it?
- what does it reveal about my assumptions?
- what is one thing I might now do differently?

The incidents allowed us to examine our beliefs. That is, by recording and examining these small happenings we began to be aware of instructional decisions that were actually interfering with our students' learning. It wasn't just the incidents alone that helped us clarify some of our assumptions. The reading we were doing and our discussion with one another affected our interpretations as well.

We were beginning to interpret our experiences in new and quite different ways.

Learning Through Teaching

Yetta Goodman's term "kid watching" captures, in part, what I'm talking about. Kid watching is the ongoing evaluation which allows continuous instructional planning. Goodman (1978) describes the way in which kid watchers are always attentive to how students are progressing, and they make decisions about what experiences and opportunities children might need in order to grow. However, our attention to students and their learning is only half of the equation. We also have to learn to see *ourselves* in the process.

Judy Mossip (1986) relates a kid-watching incident that helped her learn something new about one of her students; more important, it let her look at herself and her teaching more closely:

Amanda, a first grader, was working on a math activity. She had successfully drawn the several geometric patterns that I had begun—two circles, a triangle, two circles, a triangle, and so on. Now she was creating her own pattern row. I glanced quickly at what she was doing and could see that her row of circles didn't make a pattern. Without a pause, I pounced.

"To make a pattern you have to have more than one shape. You can't have a pattern with only one shape, Amanda."

Bravely she replied, "No, I do have a pattern—circle, oval, circle, oval, circle, oval." Amanda touched each shape as she recited her pattern, driving home her point to me.

Judy explains how Amanda's reply helped her understand that she was seeing as a teacher, comfortable with her own knowing, rather than as a learner. She realized she almost tried to force her interpretation on Amanda; however, Amanda stood her ground. "Imagine the impact of such teacher behavior on more reticent learners; shyer children might have erased their work without having any idea what they'd done wrong and been reluctant to try again."

Since I've begun exploring critical incidents with my students I've learned a lot about being a teacher myself. Let me share a couple of recent classroom incidents of my own.

I had just finished a writing conference with Greg. I'd listened to him read his piece. I'd encouraged him to talk about the difficulties he felt he was still having deciding where his writing should go. He felt the piece was unfinished and detached but he wasn't sure what to do about it. As I listened to him I recalled something he'd done with his own students which he'd described during one of our class discussions. I wondered aloud whether he mightn't actually use that experience as an opening.

"That's a possibility," he said, so I sent him off to write. Not long afterward, however, I heard him telling his group "Judith said I should. . . ."

What did I learn from Greg's comment? I was confronted with evidence of how difficult it is to step outside an authoritarian role, and it raised for me some of the problems of holding writing conferences with students. I had no clearly worked-out notion of how Greg's writing should go. I was simply trying to help him bring more of himself into the piece. I'd offered him back his own story so he could see how he'd already shared with us some incidents which illustrated what I sensed was the point of his writing. But my tentative connection had the force of a directive—not "Judith thought I might," but "Judith said I should." I'd inadvertently taken charge of Greg's writing. Only then did I realize I might have asked him whether he could think of something he'd done in his own classroom that illustrated what he was writing about and then asked him where he might use it effectively.

And yet, offering a suggestion isn't wrong either. My conversation with Debbie, which followed immediately after the conference with Greg, helped me see that. I could tell from Debbie's face and voice that she didn't feel comfortable with what she'd written. She sounded tentative and looked perplexed when I asked if she could sum up what she'd done so far:

"Tell me more about the situation," I prompted. As she talked I asked questions, I kept watching for signs of animation and authority which would let me know she was on to something. She finally began telling about her own recent experiences with writing—the furrow between her eyebrows disappeared, her face relaxed.

"Here's where she's comfortable," I thought to myself. "This is where she should be able to write. How do I help her see that?"

"Why are you hesitant to write about yourself?" I asked. She gave a couple of reasons: she didn't think her own experiences were interesting enough; besides, she thought I was expecting her to try fiction.

"Why don't you try writing the incident as a personal narrative?" I suggested. At that her face changed. I could see the tension dissipate as she left to resume writing.

This conversation made me aware that one of my roles during a writing conference, particularly when the writing is just starting out, is to help the writer make contact with what she's trying to convey. In addition, these two conversations juxtaposed allowed me to see there is no one way to assist student and teacher writers. While Debbie was able to accept a suggestion and make it her own, in Greg's case my connection was made too directly. His response to my input showed me I needed to keep out of the decision making at least until he is more willing to trust his own writing ability. Offering him the suggestion wasn't a bad thing to have done, though; it let me learn more about how to support Greg's learning and writing.

From Debbie, I also became more conscious of the need to attend to students' faces and voices during such learning/teaching moments. It was as a result of this particular conversation with Debbie that I was able to articulate what I watch for. As I described the incident in my logbook I found myself writing about her facial expression and the timbre of her voice. It was then I recognized the basis for many of my moment-to-moment teaching decisions. I was suddenly aware of how I am constantly watching students' bodies and listening to their voices in order to know how to proceed.

In the daily confusion of the classroom it's often difficult to retain some distance from what's going on, to be able to catch those moments which offer us an opportunity to be learners ourselves. And most of us, understandably, find it difficult to look at our mistakes. Yet, while we all need to find evidence that we're making headway, the most useful incidents for us as learning teachers are those which make us uncomfortable. It's only when we're able to acknowledge that the strategy didn't work or that the suggestion wasn't quite right, and then try to understand what we might have done differently, that we can begin to change and grow.

Linda Swinwood relates such a critical incident. David, a lively eight-year-old, came home from school one day with a partly written story to finish for homework:

In a few sentences he drew the story to a close. His completed story was exactly one page long.

"This is a smart story," he announced.

"Why is that?" his mother asked.

David smiled and said, "If it were any longer I'd have to recopy two pages!"

David's comment set Linda thinking. As a teacher exploring writing in new ways herself, Linda has begun to wonder about the nature and place of revision. She's seen firsthand that not everything she writes needs to be reworked. She's also discovered that revising involves a great deal more than just recopying. She's explored various ways of rearranging what she's written. On occasion she's deleted entire parts. In one instance she changed a letter into a poem as a result of having shared it. How can she help her sixth-grade students appreciate the role of revision in writing? How can she share with them some of her new revising strategies? She knows she doesn't want her students to feel as David does, satisfied to write just enough to keep her placated.

Critical incidents are easy to find once we begin looking for them. I am stumbling across them constantly. I've learned to record a couple from each class in a notebook and use them to help me examine what I'm doing. Many of my critical incidents arise from students' journal letters to me. The following situation is typical.

The teachers in one of my graduate classes were readying some short pieces of personal narrative for a class publication. They had begun with some freewriting, which had turned into short narrative stories. They had talked with one another about their writing, made revisions, conferenced again. They had just handed in what they considered to be finished pieces for me to publish. However, I became more and more uncomfortable as I read their stories. A number of the pieces really could have used another reworking. Given the time constraints of the course I felt I had two courses of action: to print the pieces as they were, or to use some of our limited time to help the teachers learn about how to craft their writing further. I chose the latter. I met with them individually and talked about their pieces with them. Some needed to learn how to eliminate unnecessary material. Others required help in clarifying their point. Still others needed stylistic assistance. Had there been more time, I might have helped indirectly by offering them some short stories that demonstrated the sort of crafting I thought they were ready to consider. As it was, I elected to be more directive and show them myself how to craft what they'd done.

That's where I ran into trouble. For several teachers, my suggestions undermined the sense of authorship I'd been working so hard to foster. Pam wrote me in her journal the following week:

> The piece of writing that really changed my opinion of myself as a writer was my fear story. I realized that by looking at a topic from a different perspective I actually had more to 'say' than I imagined. With help from my classmates I learned the importance of sharing a developing piece. On the whole I felt I had grown. Not only had I written a story, I shared it and was willing, actually eager, to revise. I liked my story. I liked me—the writer.
>
> So why do I now question "Am I a writer?" Five short minutes in class last week left me questioning my ability. I was told the story I had written could be better. Not only that, I was given no recognition for the effort or the final product. The only thing discussed in the conference was what I could (and underlying—should) change—no comment about words, phrases, descriptive passages or holding the reader's interest—things I was pleased with. My immediate reaction was to reject the suggestion for improvement that I had been given. After all this was my story.

Pam's point was well taken. Having decided to draw the teachers' attention to the matter of technical and stylistic conventions, I had overstepped some important boundaries. As I explained to Pam and the others in my next journal to them, in the total of eleven classes we would have together I was attempting to offer them a variety of writing (reading) strategies which they, in turn, could share with their students. I was trying to help them learn about writing by completing two short pieces in addition to a number of partial exploratory efforts. I was pushing for completion because one of the serious issues with which I have to contend is the assumption made by many teachers that I'm saying that spelling, grammatical, and stylistic conventions don't matter, that any writing is good enough just so long as students write. That, however, isn't true. Formal conventions such as organization, punctuation, grammar, and spelling are important; it's a matter of when and how they are addressed.

In this case, my timing was poor. I came into the writing too late in the development of the pieces. The writing had been through a couple of revisions; it was done. The teachers were pleased with their stories, as they should have been, since in the process of revising them they'd sorted out a number of technical concerns. So it was a mistake for me to attempt to use that particular writing to show them something more about crafting. What made me intervene was the fact that I could see time slipping away, and realized I might never get to the point where we would think about conventions and how to deal with them. There I was, succumbing to the pressure of not having enough time. Instead of pushing the issue, I should have moved on to the next piece of writing and become more involved in the discussions while the writing was still fluid and open. That would have been more useful for helping them think about matters relating to editing, style, and conventions. We could have used the new writing to explore how to tighten, tell more facts, or rearrange things. As it was, my suggestions took control of the writing, making some of the teachers feel what they'd done wasn't good enough, which certainly wasn't my intention.

Finding Our Way

The gap between belief and practice is always present. No matter how accomplished our teaching becomes, contradictions will occur. It's recognizing and dealing with those contradictions that make us learning teachers. I still remember a conversation I had with a colleague more than a decade ago about a new research project on literacy development I was beginning at the time. I was describing some of the reading activities we were trying with the children and outlined some of the writing activities we had developed. My colleague heard me out, and then asked, "How can you tell which activities are which?" That made me pause. "I guess I can't," I replied. "Well, then, why do you talk about it that way?"

I vividly recall the jolt I experienced at that moment. Yes, I'd been telling teachers we learn to read from reading, we learn to write from writing, but obviously I hadn't yet fully appreciated how inseparable the various aspects of language were. While I might intend that an activity focus on reading, I can't control students' engagement— they might very well be learning about writing while listening to stories, when reading them, or while relating interesting events in their lives. I was suddenly struck by the way my assumptions affect my perceptions and how my way of talking about my instructional activities offers a clue to my tacit beliefs.

Changing what we do in the classroom in any meaningful way involves changing attitudes and beliefs, but before we can change our attitudes and beliefs we have to know what they are. Don Graves (1984) describes how all of us can easily fall prey to orthodoxies. As we work with new ideas and become comfortable with new ways of teaching, we stop listening to what's going on around us, stop seeing what our students are showing us. We become complacent, thinking we have whatever change we've been trying to implement under control.

However, if I'm alert, I'm likely to find evidence that I'm not teaching what I think I am. I must accept that the learning context I attempt to create represents no more than a potential. I have no control over how students will engage with my invitations. If I look closely, I will find that they are interpreting what I'm attempting to convey in many different ways.

Our classrooms abound with orthodoxies. Rarely do we seriously question the reasons behind the way we organize the furniture, the instructional materials, or the activities unless there are problems in the classroom. However, even in a smoothly running classroom there is always a need to reflect on what's going on and to think about trying to do things differently. Maintaining a status quo works against learning. The moment we become complacent we face the danger of orthodoxy.

Transforming teaching into a learning enterprise is a journey without end. Becoming a learning teacher means recognizing that our understanding of what we'd like to have happen in our classroom and our ability to make sense of what students are trying to do will be in need of continuous revision. No sooner will some aspect of our instructional program be sorted out, than something will happen to raise further questions.

But we aren't on this journey alone. Other teachers, as well as some scholars and researchers, are fellow travelers available to offer support. "Here, have a look at this," someone may suggest, or, "Have you thought about trying it this way?" they may ask. And our students are always available to help us if we're willing to listen and to learn from them. Although we aren't on this journey alone, in the end we each have to make sense for ourselves. By engaging in dialogue with ourselves and other explorers—teachers, parents, consultants, researchers, and our students—we can each begin finding our own way.

References

Alderson, Sue Ann. 1974. *Bonnie McSmithers, You're Driving Me Dithers.* Edmonton, Alberta: Tree Frog Press.

Argyris, Chris. 1976. *Increasing Leadership Effectiveness.* New York: Wiley & Sons.

Dillon, David. 1988. "The Inservicer Inserviced: Is Your Theory Your Practice?" In *Language and Literacy in the Primary School,* ed. M. Meek and C. Mills, 263–276. London: The Falmer Press.

Goodman, Yetta. 1978. Kid Watching: An Alternative to Testing. *National Elementary Principals* 57(4): 41–45.

Graves, Donald. 1984. "The Enemy is Orthodoxy." In *A Researcher Learns to Write,* edited by Donald Graves, 185–193. Portsmouth, NH: Heinemann.

Mossip, Judy. 1986. Seeing with New Eyes. *Language Arts* 63(6): 532–533.

North, Stephen M. 1987. *The Making of Knowledge in Composition.* Portsmouth, NH: Boynton/Cook.

PART ONE

learning through teaching

Making the shift from a traditional transmission classroom to an open learner-directed environment is a difficult undertaking. It requires that we become willing to learn from our students. Adopting a learning-through-teaching stance involves risk. It means giving up security and complacency and consciously allowing ourselves to become vulnerable. Our classrooms offer us many potential critical incidents if we're prepared to look.

Albert Layton shares many of his frustrations and unanswered questions with us. His look at what is happening in his own classroom is replete with incidents that are helping him see teaching in new ways.

pat kidd, too, learned a great deal from her junior high students. By letting them take the lead, she discovered not only how to help them learn about writing, but she also became a better writer herself.

Christine Clark decided to share classroom

decision making with her grade four students. Together they wrote and produced a play, which they performed for the rest of the school and the students' parents. Christine learned a great deal from her students about how to create an open, interpretive classroom. In the process, she discovered much about helping her students conduct research.

Chris Trussler shares what she learned from five-year-old Christopher, a student in her primary class. He helped her understand that each child must find his or her own way.

Learning in
a Whole Language
Classroom
Albert Layton

After eleven years of teaching junior high science, math, and English, I moved to a grade five classroom. To my delight, I was unprepared for the energy and enthusiasm of those students. For two years I struggled—there never seemed to be enough time to keep up with the class, prepare activities, mark assignments, and supervise reading and math groups. As I began to feel more confident teaching younger students, I started to look more carefully at the what, how, and why of what I was doing.

The next year I saw many changes in my science, health, and social studies classes. Yet I was still not certain about how I should be teaching language arts, so I relied heavily on the spelling, reading, and grammar texts available to me.

In the fall of 1983, our school began a professional development project to investigate the theories of teaching writing and reading proposed by Don Murray (1980), Don Graves (1983), Don Holdaway (1979), and Frank Smith (1978). For two years we reviewed the research literature and experimented with the activities suggested by it. By then, we realized we were becoming strongly involved in whole-language-based instruction.

Indeed, I have found learning to teach in a whole language classroom to be exciting, frustrating, and challenging. I experience excitement, for example, as I watch a group of four girls decide how to read the same book so they will be able to discuss it more comprehensively. The students are encouraged to select their own books and keep a record of what they are reading. Each week I visit the groups and we discuss the strengths and weaknesses of those books. During the visit, each student reads a passage from the book to illustrate the point she is discussing. Since the reading proficiency in this group of girls ranges widely, they are struggling with the problem of selecting a story, written at a level they can all handle, that will interest all four. It becomes evident that Shannon will not be able to work on her own with the book preferred by the other three. The stronger readers agree to help her by reading orally with her.

Before the project, I would have required Shannon to struggle on her own or to select a less difficult book. This would have only frustrated her or isolated her from the rest of the group. Instead, she is enjoying the discussion about the book and is gaining valuable reading experience by working with the other readers. The girls also decide to continue with their own individual book choices in order to find other material of interest. The intensity of reading and self-motivation is far beyond anything I have seen before in my classroom.

Sometimes my excitement is mixed with frustration. While I am reviewing the concept of brainstorming to get ideas for writing material, I ask the class for a word starter. Someone offers the word "FEAR," and I begin to write words on the blackboard as ideas come to me. (See Figure 2–1.)

Thinking of a childhood friend with whom I had shared a frightening experience, I write "Jeff" on the board. Immediately J. B. interrupts, "How could Jeff scare you?" Realizing J. B. is not referring to the Jeff of my childhood memories, I reply, while pointing to the Jeff of my class, "Why do you think it is him?"

"He's the only Jeff that I know."

We begin a classwide discussion on the assumptions a reader or writer makes and the importance of details to clarify the meaning of words. The students agree that their image of Jeff changes greatly when I include his last name. Gone is the picture of a student in the classroom, and a mystery person takes his place.

During the writing time that follows, a group of boys becomes boisterous. I investigate and find them discussing their own brainstorming lists. One boy comments, "It's funny how each of us found something different that we were afraid of."

"Did you find anything you could write about?" I ask.

"Sure, all kinds of stuff!" And off they go. The discussion continues as they begin writing. Their level of engagement is far more intense than when I used to assign topics for composition. These students are writing for themselves, not just for me.

While I am experiencing this flush of success, I notice Craig sitting with a piece of blank paper in front of him. He looks very unhappy.

Figure 2-1

I ask "What's wrong?" Craig replies, "I don't know what you want me to do."

I suggest he describe what has happened in class and what he thinks he might write as a result of the activity. He finally says, "You want us to write something about ourselves."

"You've got it!" I respond, and I leave to check on another group. Later I happen to notice Craig. He still seems to be in difficulty. I inquire once more about how the writing is going and hear, "I don't know what to write about."

It is difficult to accept that Craig, who can easily produce two hundred words when he has been given a specific assignment, can have so much difficulty when left to work on his own. Why aren't the activities of the previous classes enough to develop his independence and confidence? It may be necessary to try something different with Craig, or maybe I just haven't given him enough time to work out the problem on his own. Should I try something new or should I wait? It is difficult to know just what to do.

Equally frustrating is the students' reaction when I try a different approach to a project on the provinces of Canada. I begin the social studies assignment with a number of activities I hope will encourage the class to find out more than just facts about Canada. We brainstorm about points of interest. We write about the things we would like to have in the community where we live. We talk about what we would like to see if we were to visit a particular province. We finally discuss what information we should include in a scrapbook about the provinces so a reader would know what we thought was of interest about the country we live in.

The students head for the library, where they gather information from the reference books, magazines, vertical files, and a scrap bin of old magazines the librarian keeps for cutting out pictures. Each day I am pleased with their quiet effort. However, when I look closely at their work, I see that the scrapbook has become a combination of facts, maps, and picture cutouts with little personal input from the students. I am not sure how to react when the librarian compliments me on how well my class is working in the library. She notes that they now rarely need assistance for finding information and comments on how well they are using all the resources available for their assignment. Certainly this independence is part of the growth I wanted to see, but the students seem to have ignored the activities preceding their work in the library. The scrapbooks themselves show little of the thought or development of presentation that allows a reader to see the students' reactions to what they find. Why have they completely missed this important personal aspect of the project?

This experience makes me realize that my growth as a teacher is as irregular and erratic as the growth of my students. My reading program has progressed far more rapidly and successfully than I had hoped. Although many students are showing growth in writing, I still have much more to learn about how to help those who are having difficulty. My attempts to have the students bring a more personal style into the curriculum as a whole appear to be missing key ingredients.

With every frustration I am encountering a new challenge. If I am not happy with the scrapbooks, I must find a better way to present the project so the students will put more of themselves into the reports. I know I can encourage Craig's growth in writing and nurture the development of the type of reading growth I see in the girls' group.

I also feel a whole language classroom need not stop at language-related subjects. Math and science teaching often consists of presenting concepts that are broken up instead of presenting concepts that are whole. There must be a more integrated way to explore these aspects of the curriculum. These are some of the challenges I face every day.

When I look ahead and search for ways to correct the deficiencies I see in my program or to improve on those aspects beginning to work, I find the current literature on whole language contains many valuable ideas.

Edelsky and Smith (1984), for example, have advanced the notion of "authentic writing." Authentic writing, they explain, results when the four interacting systems of language—graphophonic, syntactic, semantic, and pragmatic—are operating interactively and inter-dependently. This notion of authentic writing has made me look at the concerns I have with content writing. The children in my class were writing when they did the social studies project, but the purpose for writing was mine. I had taken from them an opportunity to discover their own authentic writing. If I'm going to encourage authentic writing, I must give the students greater freedom to select topics and presentations. I will need to provide a variety of challenges that might encourage an authentic writing response. I must be prepared to accept that the directions the students take may be different from those I had intended. However, I can also look forward to the possibility that the work will be better than anything I might have expected.

While reading Carole Edelsky's description of Karen Smith's classes (Edelsky et al., 1983), I identify several goals I would like to incorporate into my own program. I want my students to see that there is more to learning than books and school. I want them to develop their curiosity and have a desire to find out things. I want them to learn to get along with and appreciate others, be responsible for their learning environment, and have confidence in themselves.

These goals are not unique to a whole language teaching/learning perspective, but in a learner-directed classroom the probability of reaching these goals becomes greater. In an interpretive context, the students bring their own experiences into activities rather than being restricted to texts and references. With greater input into the direction of the activities, the students are required to think for themselves. This helps them develop confidence in their own decision making. In a whole language classroom, the students work *with* the teacher instead of *for* the teacher. And by working with one another, the students learn the value of cooperation.

An important, yet unexpected, aspect of trying to work from a whole language theoretical perspective in my classroom is the feeling of excitement that has returned. Each day offers me a new opportunity to grow in my understanding of learning—to grow with and from my students. Although frustrating events are frequent, even more powerful is the excitement of accepting and mastering new challenges.

I don't want it any other way.

References

Edelsky, Carole, Kelly Draper, and Karen Smith. 1983. Hookin' 'em in at the start of school in a 'Whole Language' classroom. *Anthropology and Education Quarterly* 14: 257–281.

Edelsky, Carole, and Karen Smith. 1984. Is that Writing—or are those marks just a figment of your curriculum? *Language Arts* 61: 24–32.

Graves, Donald. 1983. *Writing: Teachers and Children at Work.* Portsmouth, NH: Heinemann Educational Books.

Holdaway, Don. 1979. *The Foundations of Literacy.* Sydney: Bridge Printery.

Murray, Donald. 1980. *Eight Approaches to Teaching Composition.* Urbana, IL: NCTE.

Smith, Frank. 1978. *Reading Without Nonsense.* New York: Teachers College Press.

A Teacher
Learns How

pat kidd

October 27, 1986, Amherst, Nova Scotia. Just another annual provincial inservice? For many, perhaps—but in one workshop, the participants had chosen to be "taught" by junior high school students. Kids teaching teachers about writing. An unusual experience.

A Sustained Silent Reading period at the outset—clearly this was to be an active workshop, not a spectator inservice. The teachers, initially tentative, became engaged as they read the glossy, and often professional looking, student-crafted works. Were these full-length novels, magazines, newspapers, comic books, and plays student-written materials? An enthusiastic dialogue followed. Uncertain, yet willing, each teacher engaged in the Sustained Writing experience with its subsequent "conferencing" session. By the afternoon, a trust had replaced the initial awkwardness and the student-leaders were well in stride.

"Writing is agony," said Margie. "But I look at how I was last September—a crying mass of jelly. And now, I can say what I know aloud to anyone. I know what I'm worth and that I count. Writing my novel has helped me a lot. For me, writing is a way of thinking!"

Picking up on this last comment, Moira, the chairperson, adroitly redirected the emphasis of the workshop. "Yes, writing is important to us all—but we've come now to an even more important point. The reason we are really here." Nodding to Anne, she sat down.

From the corner group came Anne's most passionate plea: "Yes, this is what writing is. But that is only one part of it all. We've talked to you about writing but what we really want to talk to you about is *learning*. Not just *what* we have learned. But about *how* we learn. How we really learn. How we learn best."

"Well, then," John chimed in. "What is it? What exactly do you think helped us to learn last year? How *do* you learn best?" Each student in turn explained and discussed his or her own particular "how."

Sitting back observing my students, I reflected on how expertly they had discovered and outlined the "whats" of their learning. And how, even more skillfully, they had moved the center of focus to the "hows"—the process of learning. The "hows." How had we done it? How had we come this far?

Tripled images flashed to mind. The present, past, and distant past stood before me vivid and unblurred—pictures of our workshop planning sessions, pictures of our whole year's experience, and, of course, pictures of the shaky beginnings with their inevitable stops and starts.

What had we done? Thinking back, it was nothing so unusual. We had learned together. Simply that. Together we read and wrote and talked and talked and wrote and read. At times, we were faced with: "Oh, can't we please write or read this period?" No one was more selfish than I, stealing time to read a favorite novelist, write a fantasy, or have a conference when I needed it. We shared. We encouraged each other. They pulled me along. With a strange sense of complicity and collaboration, criminal-like, we stole time to pursue reading and writing and talking. As I watched the students here at Amherst, sharing the story of their learning journey, asking these teachers to engage in similar activities, I drew up images beyond the classroom: weekends devoted to planning, replanning, and refining the workshop; the heated discussions to work out its purpose; the selection of format to enhance their focus and the assessment of their audience. These were amazing pictures of ordinary kids with one purpose in mind: to entice unknown teachers to begin their own learning journeys.

And what of me—the teacher? I suppose I have a story to tell too. I embarked on a journey in learning—not apart from my students', but alongside of them. I sometimes fell a little behind, but I was always urged forward and prodded on by my students. Were you to ask me to recount that journey step by step, I wouldn't be able to do it. I kept no notes other than those to assist us with the problem at hand. I had no well-schemed plans. I let the students' needs suggest the direction, and they in turn found the solutions.

How then did I learn? Some things do stand out vividly for me— my blunders and mistakes. I did all the wrong things: fell back on the old planning, made up charts and handouts on how-to-do-this-or-that. Conferencing, I thought, needed a big buildup and long explanations. I cataloged my skimpy knowledge of it and marshaled myself to define, demonstrate, and hand out suggested conferencing questions for some classes. Happily, the charts were ignored, and the handouts remained buried within notebooks. We went about our own way of discussing, trusting, and self-evaluating. We assisted one another with tact and without intruding on the author's ownership of the piece.

The students kept me on track. They could see through the ritual and stripped away the extraneous steps simply by asking: "Why?" When I heard what they were actually saying, I too learned to ask, "Why am I doing this?" And soon we left behind these cumbersome barriers to active learning. At times, in fits of "teacherness," announcing my own personal discoveries, I would launch into a mini-lesson about the effectiveness of this or that strategy. The students would listen politely and later, even more politely, would assure me that they had already reached that point. Sustained Silent Reading and Writing, small group discussions, journals, peer and group conferencing, speaker's corner, and self-evaluation were all activities that I began to trust would help them learn. So, I did not teach "Writing." Instead, I stood back, listened, observed, and watched my students engage as writers and readers. I learned from them. Some of the time, I felt that I was redundant.

The secret, perhaps, resides in what I refrained from doing. Doing nothing is hard work. Actively standing back, giving them room, sharing control (and responsibility) with the learners, holding back and not leaping in before they can discover their own solutions were all contrary to my training. I now realize that it was not what I did as a teacher but what I did as a learner that led me to enter their circle— the author-learner circle. I shared my writing with them. I wrote with them, but I must confess: I never produced a final draft, having the courage to do no more than write for myself and my immediate writing community. Nonetheless, as a fellow writer allowed into this circle, I was accepted, afforded conferences, given encouragement, and extended support. The collegiality they awarded me was a trust, a bond that nudged me still further.

And what indeed have I learned from this year's experience with my class? Being a part of their learning journey has given me insight into students and their ability to deal with the unknown. I found that encouraging and supporting risk and exploration, allowing them to make their own mistakes, and inviting them to take the lead was not easy but it was unexpectedly fruitful.

I have also discovered that as a teacher I have to take risks too. Leaping in before you're totally ready is a necessity. And finally I learned that I had to be a learner myself. As a colearner I could see the problems firsthand and be open for new directions and solutions. In fact, doing real writing and reading and teaching was easier than I thought.

Only now, as I sit here listening to them talk about learning do I recognize the parallels with my own learning. What I need in order to learn is space, lack of pressure, immediate access to help, and time, and more time. I, too, require room to make mistakes, explorations, and discoveries. And yes, I, too, need confirmation, encouragement, and support. Most of all, I need that all-important "community of learners." In truth, I was exploring my own learning and inadvertently setting the environment and circumstances that would be conducive for me as a learner.

My learning journey, yes—but inseparable, interwoven, and even dependent upon theirs. Collaboratively we learned. They risked, and so I had to. Not through books, lectures or inservices but with my kids. That is how this teacher learned "how."

"Herb's Revenge"
Writing Our
Own Play

Christine Clark

I began by thinking about the activities in my classroom: reading, novel study, story writing, journals, message boards, etc., and how they all seemed to be working to some extent; but neither I nor the students had any strong sense about why we were doing these isolated activities. For example, when I nudged the students to consider revising some particular pieces of writing to enter in the Writer-of-the-Month contest, they frequently responded, "Why do I have to write this again?"

I began to see that the students needed to be engaged in some larger process that would make it natural for them to reconsider what they were reading or writing. I needed some kind of project that would provide a context in which it would be appropriate for students to return to whatever they were reading or writing on their own without my having to suggest it. I wanted to create a situation where the need for making their meaning clear was an inherent aspect of what was going on.

On the last Friday of every month, two classes in the school take responsibility for putting together an assembly for the rest of the students. These assemblies usually take the form of performances of one kind or another. About three months before our turn came, I began to think about some topics that might interest my thirty-one grade-four students. One of the themes in the social studies curriculum is "How Do We Learn About the Past?" I wondered whether the class might be interested in writing a historical play. I was beginning to see how such a project could provide the sort of framework I had been searching for. It would allow us to pursue a social studies theme and at the same time provide a reason for doing research, reading plays, writing, revising, rereading, editing, doing further research, and rewriting—all of which would be motivated by our need to communicate what life might have been like. As our play, "Herb's Revenge," a story set in a rural classroom of the 1930s took shape, we became very involved in using all aspects of language in order to learn about the past and communicate what we were learning to others.

Throughout the project, language was our principal tool. We read reference materials and plays, wrote letters to grandparents, read and reread their letters, talked about what we were learning, discussed how plays were written, and argued about plot and characters for "Herb's Revenge." We wrote memos and reminders to classmates and ourselves, wrote drafts of scenes, tried them out and revised what didn't work, conducted and transcribed interviews, selected pertinent information and incorporated it into the script, tried out scenes again, and revised once more. During the three months we spent researching and writing our play, we all became more effective language users.

The highlight of our efforts was the performance. The story, in which Herb, our main character, was finally caught staging pranks for which his classmates had been blamed, delighted the audience of students, teachers, parents, grandparents, and other invited guests.

Setting the Groundwork

I knew that in order for us to carry out such a project, we'd have to make some changes in our daily schedule. We needed long, uninterrupted periods of time, during which the students could pursue their search for information and also have the time required for writing. With revisions to the schedule completed, I started thinking about a way to get the project into action. I quickly realized that all activities undertaken for the playwriting would not involve all the students. The possibility for many different activities to be occurring simultaneously led me to consider my role in the classroom. I wouldn't be able to direct everyone all the time. Instead, I would have to function more as a guide. I would have to encourage the students to cooperate, share their talents, and make their own decisions. They would have to become independent. More important, they needed to trust themselves and learn the value of everyone's knowledge.

Before we undertook the project, I needed to familiarize myself with life in the past so I could better deal with some of the students' questions and direct them to appropriate sources of information. I skimmed through materials in the library, looked through school-supplied materials, investigated activities at Ross Farm (a local, historical museum), and talked to my own grandmother about her school days. Feeling somewhat prepared, I headed to the classroom and the students.

Getting Started

In January, I approached the students about writing a historical play set in a classroom of our grandparents' day for our assembly. The students accepted enthusiastically, and much discussion on how we would proceed followed. It was decided that before playwriting could begin, we needed to find out what life was like back then. We brainstormed topics that could be researched, formed interest groups, and began our search for information in books and encyclopedias from the library. In order to better understand the concept of time and the past, we accompanied our research projects with timelines of our lives, collected artifacts from our homes, and wrote our own personal history books.

After two weeks of research, we encountered several problems: limited material on chosen topics, reading difficulty of available materials, and the relevance of the research for our playwriting. After discussing these problems, we once again had to make decisions about the direction we should take. We still believed that research about the past was needed, but we had to find a new approach for acquiring information. Our discussions led us to an "obvious" solution—our grandparents.

Research on School Life During Our Grandparents' Day

Our grandparents were a rich source of information concerning the past. We wrote to them, listing specific items that we felt would be necessary to know about for our play. Letters started arriving, and the students shared what information they received. We listened to responses describing curriculum, clothing, punishment, games played, and so on; and we learned a tremendous amount about school life in our grandparents' day. A few grandparents' letters were accompanied by textbooks and pictures, which helped us enormously when we came to the building of props.

We had an abundance of material to sort through. After deciding which pieces of information were most valuable, everyone went through his or her letter, making notes. A group of four students then volunteered to put this information on a spreadsheet so we could easily examine our data. (Unfortunately, a computer was not available, so we did our spreadsheet on a large piece of paper.) From this, we discovered generalizations about the school, school life, and the people.

Learning about Plays

While waiting for replies from our grandparents, we discussed playwriting and decided we needed more information about plays. We read a number of them in an attempt to better understand their construction. After reading and discussing several plays in small groups, we discussed, together as a class, the similarities we had noticed. The students' findings, although lacking the formal terms, dealt with plot, characters, conflict, setting, sequencing of events, presenting of problem, format of writing, and so on.

Planning and Writing

Initially, small groups were each responsible for one part of the writing process: planning, writing, researching, revising, and editing.

After two days, we decided to change this setup because it did not encourage everyone's involvement in the decision making. Thus, the entire class collaborated on characters and plot. Once the events for a scene were decided upon, a group of four or five students would begin writing while the remainder of the class continued to discuss further developments in the play. When the students in each group completed a draft of a scene, they read it to the entire class, and we then decided on any necessary revisions. We didn't rewrite until the act was satisfactory. In this way, we were all involved in the entire writing process.

In the process of selecting appropriate events for the play, we returned numerous times to our grandparents' letters and our spreadsheet of notes. They became our "bible," providing information about punishment, activities in school, outside games, and prop information for clothing, furniture, and classroom setup.

As our plot took shape and the writing began we were faced with another problem—we didn't know much about a typical day's routine. This information was absent from our grandparents' letters. Knowing we had to gather some information quickly, a group of students interviewed an older teacher in the school who had attended school during the 1930s. Relying on her tape recorded descriptions, we were then able to create the activities of the students in the classroom during the school day. The daily routine was a key element needed for our writing the play, but its importance only became apparent after we had begun writing.

Memos

We found it necessary to keep a record of the props we would need for each scene as we wrote the play. The students began their lists and quickly discovered that they also had to record the function of the props. Separate groups were responsible for building props; therefore, we had to find some way of communicating the characteristics that needed consideration when those groups constructed the props. We developed a memo system for this purpose—we wrote memos concerning props information, which gave us a written record to refer to once construction began. In the first act, for example, one of the students being punished had to fill the woodstove for a week; therefore, the group responsible for building the woodstove received a memo explaining the necessity for a workable door and a place to put logs inside. Once the memo system was in operation, we realized its value and began using it to communicate about problems, helpful information, and personal messages.

Research on Props

Developing appropriate props—windows, desks, teacher's desk, potbellied stove, students' books, dunce hat, and blackboard—required new research. We returned to the library and located appropriate books and encyclopedias. We searched through our grandparents' letters and classroom kits ("When Grandma and

Grandpa Were Kids" and "January 5, 1910") and located relevant information and pictures. The students were surprised to discover that they could now take the earlier research materials that had seemed so difficult and use them effectively to gather particular information. The complexity of the reading material was no longer a problem. Because they had specific intentions in mind, they were able to skim through the materials looking for what they needed to know. The students in charge of building the potbellied stove were a perfect example of this. They no longer had to deal with all the information on potbellied stoves; they were only concerned with stoves used during the 1930s.

Final Editing, Practice Time

Finally, all acts were written and the moment of truth had arrived. Would everything fit together? During the first reading, we agreed that the sequence of events was fine and all the scenes ran together smoothly. Delighted that nothing needed revising, we prepared for our first run-through.

After several auditions, the actors were chosen and rehearsals began. It was at this point we became aware that further changes were required. The main problem involved relating dialogue to action. More dialogue was needed to cover the onstage activity. For example, there was the point where everyone onstage was waiting expectantly for a student's outburst as he sat on a tack. We added a few lines to fill the space. As soon as the revisions were done, our efforts went into polishing our performance.

Performing

On the day of the assembly we waited nervously for our cue. Out into the gym went Herb and Miss Bower, the characters in the opening scene. The play was underway! The students' improvisations brought the play to life. Our performance, before a group of seventy parents and grandparents along with 320 fellow schoolmates, was a huge success.

Reflections

Writing "Herb's Revenge" involved us in many valuable learning experiences. For us, playwriting became a legitimate task in order to meet our responsibilities for the assembly. Every activity we undertook contributed to that end in some way. When we ran into problems, we discussed our difficulties and didn't hesitate to discard a particular strategy and look for a better way to get something done.

The project required the development of a sense of community where everyone was responsible for his or her part. The collaboration I witnessed among the students came about not because I dictated it but because the students had a need to communicate problems, insights, or information that would prove helpful in reaching our final goal. They didn't need me to tell them what to do next. They were able to work toward accomplishing their objectives and made any necessary decisions on their own. They often needed support and guidance with their decisions, but the decision making rested on their shoulders. Sometimes we made a wrong decision, but we did not give up or view it as failure. It was just another step in our learning, all of which contributed to a successful outcome.

I was also a learner throughout this project. I was concerned about my role in the organization of the project; they with the task of writing the play. Together we learned from our mistakes and came to understand their importance for learning. My most relevant insight deals with the preparatory research we undertook before we began writing the play, because I realized that only after we actually began the writing did we know exactly what it was we needed to know. Our most useful research was done after we began writing. No amount of preliminary research could prepare us for the problems that arose when we were in the middle of writing our play. I learned that we need to get into the "meat" of things quickly, and then worry about what we need to know as problems arise.

The importance of using language for learning cannot be overemphasized. Language is our tool for communication, and through it we learn. It allows us to make sense of the world around us outside of school. It is through the natural occurrence of problems in our daily lives that we become involved in solving problems. We do what is required in order to solve those problems, and we learn from our successes and mistakes. We deal with complex information in our attempt to make sense of the world around us because we stand to benefit personally. Why should learning be different in the classroom?

5

Learning From Christopher
Journal Writing With Five-Year-Olds
Chris Trussler

We had gathered on the rug to share our writing for the day. Each of my primary students was given the opportunity to share what he or she had written. As usual, some were more eager than others, and certainly none was more eager than Christopher. He insisted he read first, and he approached the writer's chair with great ceremony, announcing, "I have worked six long days on this story!" He read to us of his dream—a dream in which he believed his mother had been killed, only to find her in the shower. Christopher's nightmare had affected him deeply, and his writing about it seemed to have a cathartic effect. As he returned to his place in the circle he rejoiced in the completion of his story, and I secretly rejoiced that he had finally accepted my invitation to join what Frank Smith (1983) refers to as the "club" of writers.

There were many times during the previous months when I was afraid that Christopher would never accept my invitation to engage in writing. I had met him the spring before he entered my primary class and found him to be quite bright and comfortable in the classroom. What a surprise when he arrived the first day! There were no tears at first, only silent noncompliance. In spite of my encouragement, Christopher spent the first morning of school at his table. Urging him to participate did little but provoke floods of tears—not the whiny tears of an uncooperative child, but quiet, sobbing tears of terror.

The second day began with promise. Although Christopher was still not a willing participant in singing or shared reading, he reluctantly joined the circle, and we made it through most of the morning without any tears. However, terror returned when I began to talk about writing.

This was the first year that I was inviting my primary children to write before Christmas. I'd read numerous articles and books that supported my decision; however, nothing had prepared me for the reaction I received from Christopher and several other children. Despite the openness of my instructions, "Draw or write about anything you would like," "I'll help you with your story," etc., Christopher refused to put pencil to paper.

As he sat at his table, his huge brown eyes blinking back tears yet again, I was tempted to put the journals away until January. I decided instead to let him face the empty page. Thirty minutes later, after much encouragement, Christopher had drawn me a picture of himself and had written, "I AN CHRIS." Relieved, he handed me his journal. I was excited with his efforts and invited him to tell me about his story. Silence. His job was done. He had written in his journal and was not about to take further risks by talking about his work.

During the days that followed, I became increasingly concerned with Christopher's refusal to participate in our writing activities. Each morning as the children discussed what they were going to write about, Christopher sat silently, refusing to look at either the children or me. Each day I passed him his journal; each day he returned to his seat to weep, not to write. I offered to help him, even write for him, but he said nothing. Toward the end of the first week, we gathered on the rug to talk about the news of the day, and I suggested to Christopher that he might like to write about some of the things we had been discussing. Tears began again and he sobbed, "I just can't do that today."

Again I asked myself why I was putting Christopher through this agony. As I handed him his journal and looked at his tear-streaked face, I tried to reconcile his terror with the openness of my invitation. I was asking the children to write or draw on a topic of their own choice—an activity that took maybe twenty minutes. When they were finished, they would share their stories with me or with a friend. I usually responded to their journals with a written comment, which we would read together. Never once did I say that I expected the spelling should be correct or that they should take care to print neatly in their journals. If anything, the message I was trying to convey was the opposite—I wanted them to see the focus of the journal writing to be on meaning.

Yet I discovered that Christopher and several other children in my class were hesitant to write any word they couldn't spell correctly. I was astonished that they had come to school with this expectation already firmly established. This was the first lesson I learned from Christopher, and the strategies he used for coping with this expectation instructed me further in how to provide these children with the choices that would help them over this important hurdle.

Despite my continual reassurances that I wanted them to spell words as they believed they were spelled, it was months before Christopher and some of the other children were confident enough to invent spelling. The articles I had read about "first-grade" writing had prepared me for scribble writing and writing that only the child could decipher, but it hadn't prepared me for the situation I was facing with Christopher. I was expecting to hear stories based on personal experiences, yet day after day Christopher would copy from the stories and poems we had been sharing, or he would repeat the same sentence, with only minor modifications, for days. I wasn't sure how to respond to his writing. I was so pleased that he was writing anything that I praised his efforts, all the while encouraging him to talk and write about his own experiences.

As December approached, Christopher continued to resist my invitation to invent spelling. Throughout the year I had encouraged collaboration among peers. It was in December that Christopher discovered Jeffery and Justin could spell many of the words he might need to spell, and he hounded them persistently until they would finally tell him to "figure it out [himself]." Christopher also realized that there were certain times when I would spell words for him, and he would often ask at the beginning of a writing period if I would be "walking around" that day. I usually responded to this implied invitation for assistance by walking around, listening and responding to what the children were writing, rather than working on my own journal.

The end of January and second term report cards approached, and I continued to be concerned about Christopher's reluctance to spell functionally. It was Christopher's nightmare that seemed to be the turning point in his willingness to engage in the writing process. He had a story to tell, and, for the first time, his strategies for avoiding functional spelling weren't sufficient. As he wrote the story he scanned books for the words he needed, grilled classmates, and toward the end he actually took the risk to try and spell words for himself. To an outsider the product would not appear spectacular, but to Christopher it was a story that had taken, as he put it, "six long days to write." He was still concerned with correctness, but he had experienced the power of writing and the excitement of sharing a story with others.

As I reflect on these past few months, I realize that Christopher's reluctance to write forced me to rethink how I believe writing should be taught to primary children. Christopher helped me see that children may not respond immediately to my invitation to join the "club" in spite of how nonthreatening I try to make the invitation. In the end, Christopher had to decide to take his own risks. The copying and days of monotonous repetition in Christopher's writing were a necessary part of his becoming confident enough with the writing process to chance writing about personal experiences. There is evidence of his gaining control of the process in his comments to me about whether I would be "walking around." Christopher was in effect saying, "Look, I need your help today, so please be available."

My experience with Christopher has helped me reflect on my role in a writing classroom. In the face of children who are reluctant to engage in writing, my role is to continue to advance the invitation and to allow them the choices that will encourage them to take control of the writing process. In Christopher's case, I saw the power of his finding a subject, a story that he desperately needed to tell. Through Christopher's struggle I also became aware of the need to encourage peer interaction and to be sensitive to covert calls for assistance. Yet the most powerful lesson I learned from Christopher is that a five-year-old can indeed teach me about teaching methodology. I need only listen and watch closely.

Reference

Smith, Frank. 1983. Reading like a writer. *Language Arts* 60: 558–567.

PART TWO

making connections

Many important insights about learning and teaching occur outside of the classroom. Everyday experiences, many apparently insignificant events, afford us opportunities to make connections with what we're doing as teachers. However, little learning can occur unless we take notice of these moments. Making the connection between events in our out-of-school lives and what's happening in our classrooms is an important aspect of becoming a reflective, learning teacher.

Becoming a reflective practitioner holds many surprises, not all of them comfortable. Murray Wickwire shares an incident with a young friend that forced him to examine some of his writing instruction practices. He realizes that important insights about how to help his students write have come from his having become a writer himself.

Beth Valentine also relates how becoming a writer and sharing her writing with others in the class has helped her make unexpected connections about the social, collaborative nature of the writing enterprise—connections she sees influencing how she teaches writing.

Evelyn Bent describes three critical incidents that together helped her ask some important questions about control in learning situations. As she explores an unsuccessful learning experience of her own she sees the necessity for allowing learners to be involved in some of the instructional decision making.

Janet Ripley recounts an experience involving her daughter that allows her to make new connections about the value of hands on experience for learning.

Why Teachers Must be Writers
Murray Wickwire

The other day I made my regular stop on the way home from school to visit a young friend. I climbed the stairs to find thirteen-year-old Greg trying to sort out the various projects and assignments to be done for school the next day.

Greg, now in eighth grade, is a good student. He works hard to maintain high grades. However, much of our after-school time I spend listening to him complain about the homework he has to do each evening. On this particular afternoon I found Greg more frustrated than usual. He was sitting amid a big pile of books and papers on his bedroom floor. He was very distraught. With exams approaching, he needed time to study, but he was inundated with assignments for the next day.

The computer was on, and I could tell that Greg was working on something. I glanced at the screen and recognized an essay he'd recently completed.

"You're working on that English essay again? I thought you'd finished it," I said.

"I handed it in but my teacher wanted the rough copy too," Greg replied.

"Mmhmm." I nodded.

"Well, I didn't really have a rough copy to pass in. I mean, I tried explaining to my teacher that I used the computer to write my essay. I wrote it, made changes and corrections, and then saved and printed it," said Greg.

That seemed reasonable to me. I wondered why he was having to work on it again. "And what did your teacher reply?" I asked.

"Well, my teacher wouldn't accept my explanation. He said I had to have a rough copy," Greg told me. "I tried to tell him what I had done, but he wouldn't listen to me. He said if I didn't have a rough copy to hand in with my good copy, I wouldn't get a mark for it at all."

"So what did you do next?" I asked.

Greg went on. "Well, I asked him what I was supposed to do, and he said if I didn't have a rough copy I would just have to make one up to pass in with the essay."

My eyes opened wide in surprise. "He didn't really tell you to do that, did he? Are you sure that's what he told you to do?"

"Why do you think I'm working on it again?" Greg asked me.

No wonder Greg was so upset. Here was this thirteen-year-old struggling to recreate an earlier version of a completed piece of writing. He was deliberately misspelling words, making grammatical errors, and rearranging paragraphs in his essay. Seeing his distress, I decided to give him a hand so he could finish the assignment and move on to other homework.

Helping Greg recreate his rough draft was an eye-opener for me. Until that moment I hadn't appreciated how difficult it is to deliberately write something badly. Together we made a variety of changes in the writing and then printed out a copy. Once we had a printout, we worked through the writing, sentence by sentence. We carefully penciled in corrections above the mistakes we'd inserted. We drew lines indicating changes in paragraph arrangement. We circled words and wrote in the correct spelling. We restored the punctuation we'd removed. When we were done, we printed out the previous "good" version and checked it against the current rough copy—we wanted to make sure we'd covered our tracks. Now, we had a "good" copy accompanied by a "rough" draft.

At that point I asked Greg if he had had any opportunity to share his draft before reworking it. He told me he hadn't and that both the draft and the completed essay were to be passed in together.

I was more frustrated and exasperated than Greg was by the time we were finished, I think. I had stayed much longer than I had expected. As I trudged up the driveway to my car, I shook my head in disbelief at what we had just done together.

In the days that followed, I thought about some of the assumptions about writing and learning that Greg was having to deal with. There are three that stand out for me. The first is that growth in writing can be judged by the difference between a single rough copy and a final version. A second is that collaboration and responding to work in progress is unimportant to the development of writing. The third is that the computer is not an acceptable writing tool.

While I used to hold these assumptions myself, having become a writer recently has helped me see writing differently. For example, I have come to understand the complexity of the growth of writing. In my own recent writing experience, revising is vital to the development of my writing. I am constantly rethinking and reworking what I want to say. My writing is nonlinear in its development. The first draft does not necessarily lead to a second, more improved attempt. Much of what I want to say never makes itself evident in a single rough copy but happens after a number of tries. It is through a revision process that meaning evolves for me. Once I have the ideas sorted out, I can then attend to editing, working on details like punctuation and format. There was nothing in his writing experience to help Greg's writing evolve. The changes we made were largely surface ones.

Sharing my writing has also become important. Having a chance to freewrite and share with fellow writers helps give focus and direction to my ideas. This collaboration provides an opportunity for other people to respond to my writing and allows me to ask them questions and work out problems. For Greg there was no collaboration, no reason to develop his ideas further or to examine the coherence of his argument. He wasn't writing to inform readers he cared about; he was writing for a grade.

The computer also plays an important role in the development of a piece of writing. It has helped my fluency tremendously. The drudgery of erasing and rewriting is made much easier. I can move blocks of text back and forth effortlessly. I can insert text in places where I feel I want to say more or say something differently. My computer has made the whole process much easier and has let me come to enjoy writing rather than avoid it. Writing on the computer, however, proved to be a liability for Greg.

My experience with Greg has made me take a careful look at the writing I'm doing with my own fifth graders. Having become a writer myself, I have a better understanding of the kinds of decisions writers have to make. Becoming aware of the role of revision and of the value of sharing writing in progress has made a major difference in the writing done in my classroom. First of all, I write with my students. We spend a good deal of time putting ideas on paper. We also spend an equal amount of time talking about the writing in pairs, small groups, or as an entire class. We share beginnings and endings. We talk about writing in different genres and share books and stories that suggest ideas and provide examples. We read our writing numerous times and take time to ask questions and work out problems. And we celebrate the publication of finished work. Since we don't have computers to write with, we often talk about other ways of making writing easier. I offer suggestions and strategies for making revisions and for editing.

My role in all of this is to provide a rich and inviting environment where students will want to write and learn. I encourage my students to select their own topics and to make decisions about how to proceed. I set expectations I think the students are capable of meeting. These may not be the same expectations for everyone.

Becoming a writer has helped me become a better writing teacher. I am more aware of the assumptions that direct what I do in the classroom. Nevertheless, situations and problems that challenge what I have come to believe about how to help students learn to write constantly occur. Today one of the students, Jack, began a "choose your own adventure" story. When I asked him to share what he'd written, he read a full page copied from his favorite "choose your own adventure" book. I wasn't sure at that moment how to help him out. I have never tried writing a "choose your own adventure" story myself. I can see I will have to have a short go this evening. Then, tomorrow when Jack and I chat, I'll be in a better position to ask him about what it is he's trying to do. Maybe we'll try writing an original story together. One thing I do know—I won't ask him to recreate a rough draft of his work.

Simply, "Margot"
Beth Valentine

For the last three years, I had been grappling with some major questions about children and how they learn to write. I had been observing my students and asking myself if all this drafting, editing, conferencing and publishing was really necessary. I hadn't found many satisfactory answers on my own, and so I enrolled in a graduate course where I am learning about children as writers by becoming a writer myself. Every Tuesday I have clutched my bulging writing folder and climbed the four flights of stairs in the hopes that this will be the week I discover the answers.

Recently, I arrived for class in my usual disheveled state, plopped my folder down on the table, exchanged greetings with the other members of my group, and tried to catch my breath in the few remaining minutes before class started. I felt a nudge at my elbow. It was Linda—she handed me a note, which was a response to my piece of writing in our recently published class collection. My story had described an incident with a young boy whose teacher had insisted he have all his homework signed by his parents. For me, the story was about trust and responsibility. I had identified with the child's indignation at his teacher's blatant lack of trust and for the first time recognized myself in the classroom. In a matter of minutes a second note found its way into my hand. Second response! I felt a sense of wonder.... there were two people in this class who wanted to tell me how my writing had affected them.

Linda described how she, too, identified with this incident and liked the way I illustrated the relationship between me and my students. I hadn't thought about that comparison much when I had written, but her comments made me think about why I had made those particular choices.

The second note was neatly typed on a small slip of paper and was signed simply, "Margot."

53

I read the lines quickly, backtracked, and read them again. What was she saying about my writing? She liked the piece, but found it cold. This really set me thinking. Her comment made me reconsider what I'd written. She felt that I had distanced the reader from the piece by jumping back and forth between scenarios. I thought about that. I hadn't intended the piece to be cold. Suddenly, I was looking at my writing from an entirely different perspective.

During the class, I shared Margot's response with the other members of my group. I wanted their reactions to my writing too. Margot's response had captured my attention and I wanted to pursue her perception with the others. Janice disagreed with Margot; she hadn't thought the piece cold at all. Murray agreed with Janice. But Brian supported Margot's contention. He admitted he had not read beyond the first paragraph the first time through the collection, but later he'd returned and read the whole thing. As we discussed my story, I sat back in utter amazement that one piece of writing could affect four people so differently.

I glanced at Margot's response and in that moment I realized that here lay the embodiment of my quest. When viewed alone, it didn't seem such a significant event, but for me it was a very important piece of the writing puzzle. I had finally made a connection between what Frank Smith (1983) describes of learning to write and my own experiences.

. . . the first responsibility of teachers is to show children that writing is interesting, possible and worthwhile. But there is also no way of helping children to write if the teacher does not think that writing is interesting, possible and worthwhile. Teachers who are not members of this club cannot admit children to this club. How can teachers learn to see themselves as writers? They must learn to write as writers themselves, and to do that they must, like children, collaborate with people who are also engaged in the enterprise of writing . . . as members of the club THEY will learn (p. 566).

Margot had given me more than just her opinion of my work. She had helped me to read as a writer! Her sharing of her response with me had forced me to view my own writing with different eyes. I was now seeing how the sharing of my writing was an essential element in learning about how to be a writer. Never having received genuine feedback before, how could I possibly understand the value of responding to writers and receiving responses? I had been teaching writing without being a writer myself. It's little wonder I had such unsatisfactory results. I didn't understand the process! By being responded to, my writing was no longer a private act. I had now become aware of my audience; I began to write with them in mind. I saw my writing as something that I would eventually share, and this changed how I viewed what I wrote. I realized it no longer belonged to me the minute someone else read it. I stopped feeling defensive. Others were entitled to react. I could now see how much their insights aided me as a writer.

I have learned so much from my fellow students that I can't understand why we insist that writing be a solitary event in school. A teacher can only chat with so many students each day. Besides, no matter how supportive my professor's comments, they never held the impact that input from classmates did. The other students could often see where an idea started to fall apart or an argument lost its sense of direction when I couldn't. They shared insight they had gained from their own student/teacher conferences, things the professor had forgotten to mention to me, or that had simply never come up in our discussions. My conversations with fellow writers instilled in me the desire to continue writing even when my writing seemed so hopeless. I wrote to try out their suggestions, for their reactions—not to please a teacher or fulfill an assignment.

I now appreciate that we learn best what we learn from each other. Peer conferencing has taught me that. And responding. I saw how motivated I became when I received encouragement from the others in my group. I had a purpose for writing. I had an audience. I can understand now why it is so important that children have this same support.

There will be changes in the future in the way I teach. Writing will be something that we all participate in—I intend to stay a writer! I want my students to feel the same commitment to their writing that I have to mine, and this can only happen when they have been given the opportunity to become involved with one another's writing.

Reference

Smith, Frank. 1983. Reading Like a Writer. *Language Arts* 60(5): 558–567.

8

Who Should Have Control?

Evelyn Bent

"Mom, I was born to learn," my five-year-old son Colin said to me one day recently while we were making lunch together. We had been discussing how well his swimming had been coming, and he was eager to tell me about his move to the large pool. Although the family had extended him numerous invitations to join us in the deeper water, he had been content to play for hours in the small pool discovering how to swim, float, and do front and back somersaults. He hadn't had any formal swimming lessons because we believed that he would learn, given the opportunity and plenty of time in a supportive climate. We had played with him in the shallow water and held him until he indicated we were no longer needed or wanted. We continued to offer encouragement, and Colin, feeling successful and in control, continued to learn.

So why was I surprised Colin viewed himself as a learner? At first I think I was surprised that a five-year-old could articulate how he felt about himself. It also made me look at what was happening to Colin at school. I was concerned that Colin's teachers wouldn't help him sustain his belief in his own learning capacity.

The other day when I asked Colin if he would like to write a story for me, he hedged. He had only learned up to q so far, he said. The teacher hadn't yet shown him how to make z. I asked him if he thought he might need the letter z in his story. "No," he replied, "but I can't write a story until I can write all the letters." I thought about his comment. What did it say about what he had learned about learning in school? Although Colin has recognized the letters of the alphabet since he was two, could recite them in order by the time he was three, and has been writing ever since, he has learned in a few short months of school that he can't write a story until the teacher says he's ready.

This contrast between Colin's view of himself as a swimmer and as a storywriter concerns me. It looks as if Colin has discovered that when he is in control of his own learning, he can learn anything he wants to. When the teacher is in control, his progress is in her hands. In school he is learning to rely on his teacher to tell him what and when to learn.

How *do* people learn? I was asked to think about this question in one of my graduate classes this past year. When I examined my own learning I was surprised at what I uncovered. There were many things I had learned successfully: playing basketball, cooking, making bread, playing bridge, sewing. Perhaps I could focus on how I learned to make bread. I recalled watching my mother in the kitchen mixing and kneading the dough. We were a large family, so she made bread daily. One of us was always beside her at the kitchen counter, hands covered in flour, helping. I also remember baking bread with a partner in home economics class. This opportunity helped consolidate what I already knew. However, I didn't know I could make bread until I tried it on my own.

Shortly after I was married, I bought a book on bread making and read the instructions. Understanding the information was easy. I visualized the experience in my mother's kitchen and mentally went through the steps involved. I made repeated attempts, trying different recipes for different kinds of bread. My husband supported my efforts by eating the failures as well as the successes. There was lots of support from friends who also enjoyed the results.

What did thinking and writing about my learning to make bread help me discover about learning? I realized I had had demonstrations of bread making from my mother, the home economics teacher, and from the authors of the books I used to help me understand the process. I had encouragement from my husband and friends. My failures were learning experiences that made me want to try again. I had initiated the interest and had a desire to learn. The results of my repeated attempts were accepted and helped me gain confidence in my bread-making ability. But more than that, I was in control of the learning situation; I decided when I was ready to try something unfamiliar or difficult.

I found thinking about something I failed at more difficult. (Could it be we tend to put unpleasant memories out of mind?) French. The one word brings a rush of anxiety. It wasn't that I didn't want to learn French. I did and still do. Why didn't I learn to speak the language with any fluency?

In seventh grade we had a Francophone teacher. In fact, he could hardly speak any English. This should have been a good learning situation, but the teacher had discipline problems (one of them was me), and I spent more time outside the class than in. His concept of teaching French was to offer us a series of words to memorize, recite, and spell. We were tested almost daily. I had little opportunity to use the words in any meaningful way; I only wrote them on tests. I persevered through the next five years of French classes doing written translations of easy French passages. This was useful for passing exams but not for becoming a fluent speaker. However, other people seemed to learn to speak French with this kind of instruction, so I figured I had a problem learning languages.

In university, I was required to take a second language. I probably should have tried Spanish or German. I persisted with French. The university class had twenty-five students. I remember only one: she wanted to practice her French. She and the professor had great conversations; I understood none of what was said. I would walk to class reciting memorized passages from French writers and philosophers that made no sense to me. When I was called upon to recite in class, my mind would go blank. Working in the language lab was no better. Trying to answer a disembodied voice I didn't understand was agony.

Although my transcript records that I passed the equivalent of second-year university French, I know I really failed. I cannot speak the language and have only minimal competence reading and writing it.

The desire to learn was there, the teaching materials were in place, and there were people willing to help. Why didn't I learn? I now realize I never had the opportunity to use the skill I was supposed to be learning in any meaningful context, and so I seldom experienced success. The problem was multifaceted. The teachers believed that if they could break down the language and feed it to me in small bits, I would learn. And I believed that if I did exactly what they told me to do, I would succeed. I placed the control of my learning in their hands. My continual difficulty undermined any belief that I could really learn successfully.

How does Colin's learning to swim, my learning to bake bread, and my failure to learn French fit together? They have helped me reflect on the learning process and have given me some insight into why I am concerned about what and how my son is learning in school.

People, children as well as adults, learn when the learning is embedded in a real, meaningful situation. In such circumstances, learning is natural and easy. People learn best when they're spurred on by their keen desire to make sense of their world and to communicate that sense to others around them. We learn best in a supportive setting where others are interested and excited about sharing in our learning. We willingly take risks when the cost of failure is minimal. We will try again when there is encouragement and some sense of control over what and how we're learning.

As Colin demonstrated, children see themselves as learners. They will continue to see themselves as learners if we as parents and teachers offer opportunities for them to discover more about their world and their place in it. In our effort to help them learn, we must be careful not to take control of the learning out of their hands.

**But You Haven't
Done Any
Research**

Janet Ripley

What a dismal, wet day. I felt caged in. For two weeks I had squirreled myself away in the local library, researching a term-paper, "The Value of Hands-On Learning," but today, as I sat in my kitchen, I couldn't settle down to write.

"Hey, Mom, look at the birdfeeder. The male purple finch keeps pushing the female away," shouted Vicki, my nine-year-old. "Why is he being so mean?"

Looking through the kitchen window, I thought back six months to the day Vicki had built her feeder, using an ice-cube tray with a tinfoil pie plate for the roof, and had tied it to the maple tree. "Don't be disappointed dear, if the birds don't come. Remember last year? They went everywhere but here," I cautioned.

"I know," she said, "but I want to work on my bird-watcher's badge for Girl Guides, so I have to make a feeder. Gerald said to get mixed birdseed."

Our neighbor, Gerald, always has a yard full of sparrows, so at the grocery store I picked up a small bag of the seed he suggested. Vicki filled the feeder every morning before catching the school bus. It didn't hold much. As I had predicted, birds continued to avoid our yard. I have to give Vicki credit for her persistence. Even though only two mouthy blue jays appeared, she regularly tended the feeder.

Several weeks later, she asked, "What's that little bird? Look, there's another. Oh, another just flew off. They have black heads. Do you know, Dad?"

"Well, I think they're chickadees," he replied. "I wonder if they'll stay long."

They not only stayed, but multiplied. One morning, after filling the tray, Vicki announced, "Two of the chickadees look different. I call them Herbie and Rose. See Herbie walking down the tree trunk near the feeder?"

Sure enough. There was a different-looking bird, not a chickadee at all. As we watched, Herbie took a sunflower seed and flew off to a nearby branch to break open the shell.

"They only eat the sunflower seeds," said Vicki. "I have to dump the rest out of the feeder every few days." The next week I picked up a bag of pure sunflower seeds for her project.

She continued the morning feeding but at about two in the afternoon, the maple tree seemed alive as birds waited for Vicki's return from school. They wanted supper. Every week, I seemed to be buying more seed.

Coincidentally, Vicki received a copy of *A Field Guide to Birds East of the Rockies* from Santa. It's amazing how perceptive he is! Herbie and Rose were there—red-breasted nuthatches. The bird in the diagram was even walking down a tree just like Herbie.

"Put out these heels of bread when you feed the birds today," I suggested, after cleaning out the bread box. "Someone may like them." That was the beginning of a steady flow of table scraps finding its way to the foot of the maple. Vicki's brother suddenly developed the habit of leaving at least one bite of food on his plate so she would have something to take out. She did not always appreciate this kindness.

One blustery day, school was canceled. No one wanted to leave the house, but Vicki donned my boots and her brother's coat and trudged through the snow to her feeder. No sooner was she back in the house than the tree was buzzing.

"What are they? They're bigger than chickadees, and yellow, and there must be . . . twelve, thirteen, fourteen at least." Vicki had our attention.

"Those are evening grosbeaks. They must have lost their bearings in the storm," answered her father. "I've never seen so many." They stayed only a short while, but returned about once every two weeks after that.

We were soon glued to the window the morning Vicki asked, "What birds are red?" Three beautiful reddish-purple-headed birds were perched near the feeder while a dozen or so brownish-striped birds waited nearby.

"Get the bird book," I shouted. We found two possibilities, and after a week's observation we were pretty sure they were purple finches.

"Some of the brownish birds are small. Do you think they are babies?" asked Vicki.

"February seems an odd time to have babies. What do they look like?" I asked.

"They have some yellow on their wings and they like to eat on the ground," came the reply. We sat down and leafed through the book: pine siskins, another kind of finch. I'd never even heard of them.

Today, Vicki made another announcement. "Some of the little birds have yellow heads and white stripes on their wings." Now, what could they be? Back to the book—American goldfinches in their winter plumage.

"Are you going to write your paper now, Mom? I'll sit down with you and write my bird report," said Vicki.

"But you haven't done any research . . ." I began, before realizing my own stupidity. She had been observing birds, their feeding habits and preferences, their songs, flight patterns, and social behavior for six months.

"I bet my report will be as long as yours, Mom. I have so many things to write about." Suddenly, so had I. Together we happily passed the rest of that no longer dismal, wet day.

PART THREE

---

questioning assumptions

The difficult part of becoming a learner-directed teacher is learning to see the beliefs that undergird our instructional decisions. Every teaching act, every decision we make in the course of the day, every response in the classroom, is based on a number of often contradictory assumptions. We function intuitively, partly because there is rarely enough time to consider the implications of our actions at the moment when we are responding; our assumptions remain unexamined partly because the lore of teaching focuses our attention on the "how-to"s instead of the "why"s.

The three articles in this section show teachers beginning to ask themselves "why?" Fred Williams holds a conversation with himself—he reflects on some of his assumptions about teaching writing. He shows how his experiences in a collaborative writing context helped him change how he views writing instruction.

Marion Anderson takes a critical look at

some of her fears about being a teacher. She raises crucial questions about control and responsibility.

In "That First Year Back," Florence Kanary shares how her students helped her question some of her beliefs about learning and teaching. She describes how she has come to terms with some of her concerns about what happens in a learner-directed classroom.

Looking Back
Fred Williams

Teaching is like a wilderness trek: the terrain is difficult, the direction uncertain, and the focus is always on the trail ahead. But the top of a hill or a shady brook offers a moment to rest and reflect on the trail behind. Part of my journey was a study leave, and one stop along the way set up a mental dialogue that helped me examine what I learned about writing and being a writing teacher.

Self 1: Well then, tell me about your year. What have you learned? How did it all begin?

Self 2: I think for teachers, change has its roots in those frustrating moments when we ask, "What are we really teaching?" There was one day in particular. I had spent the evening correcting essays written by my grade-nine students, and I remember thinking how little investment the students had made in their writing. It's not that the students didn't have time to do a good job: I gave them a month. But I knew most of the assignments had been done the night before. When some of the kids looked at the mark on their papers and filed them in the garbage, I knew something was wrong. It seemed as if I cared more about the writing than the kids did. If I cared so much, why didn't I want to see it while in progress?

Self 1: Isn't that the way writing has always been done? Can it be any different? Kids write their last-minute essays and we mark them. Those with good marks keep their papers and the others . . . well, you know where they go. They don't like to write and there's not much we can do about it.

Self 2: It's not like that in every classroom. I saw a different attitude toward writing in the elementary school. One day I went to Mrs. Fraser's class and saw the students writing in their journals. They were very absorbed in what they were doing; Mrs. Fraser was writing too. Nobody noticed as I walked around the room. Even Rocky, the kid who usually bounced off the walls, was writing! Contrary to the usual "be-quiet-and-write-by-yourself" scene, which I so often tried to create in my grade nine classroom, here the kids were in groups reading their pieces or helping each other with writing conventions. A few worked on their own.

As a resource teacher, I saw this same enthusiasm in students from other elementary classrooms. Sometimes the kids in my resource program brought their journals to work on or to read. I then began to see some differences in the way writing was approached: these writers were writing for themselves. They enjoyed doing it and were given support as they wrote. They wanted to share. Why didn't my grade-nine students feel the same?

Self 1: Surely you don't believe that writing at the elementary level is the same as writing at the junior/senior high level. It's play compared to the serious tasks given in secondary school. Besides, elementary teachers don't have to mark the writing, and that makes a difference. I don't see that the two experiences are in any way the same.

Self 2: I used to believe that. It wasn't until late in the year I could say to myself that writing was essentially the same for everybody. It wasn't only journals the kids enjoyed doing, it was every task that had some meaning for them. Audrey, a grade-two student, was writing an essay on moose because one had wandered into her yard that morning, and she wanted to know more about it. Audrey and the other elementary students were researching, responding to issues, and doing personal writing, and it was authentic. Their writing was evaluated more than graded, but the teachers were still concerned about regular reporting and end-of-year promotion.

Self 1: You said a minute ago that writing was evaluated more than graded: aren't they the same?

Self 2: I've learned that evaluation and grading are not the same thing. Grading is an arbitrary letter or number assigned to represent "progress," generally based on a product or task. When I corrected the grade-nine essays I expected to see an even, linear development of writing skills. I rarely got it, because I judged the piece on how closely the writing met conventional expectations. I was grading the product. I now see that evaluation reflects the context. I should consider the intentions of the writer as well as my expectations. Evaluation can also account for the writer's ability and willingness to take risks. My practice of assigning writing topics and correcting the first draft ignored these crucial concerns.

Self 1: What else helped you form this view of evaluation and grading?

Self 2: Mostly it was by being in a class of teachers who were trying to make sense of the writing process. A profile of our "Writing and Computers" class would have revealed a group of writers with average abilities—some more or less willing to take risks—and a teacher who also struggled with grading. Evaluation happened all the time, but she tried to keep it separate from grading. Nevertheless, all the complexities of grading were there: should grading be based on present ability, as varied as it is in every class, or represent the perceived gains within the framework of the experience? In the end it seemed more the latter, since we had an opportunity to determine our grade if we chose. Who better to know than the learner? That, along with the teacher reading our weekly journals and helping with our personal writing, showed me that grading can also be a collaborative enterprise.

Self 1: As I listen to you I have a sense that you didn't come to these conclusions all at once or because of one experience. Would this change have happened in the normal course of your career?

Self 2: The whole issue of professional development is complex. I can only give you my perspective. I wouldn't have come to these conclusions if I had remained in my former situation. I had to take another direction, to have another look at theory and practice. Shifts were occurring in learning theory in terms of how and why we read and write, but they were having little impact on me. I heard about them at inservices, but that wasn't enough to invite me to rethink my beliefs.

Self 1: But what direction must a teacher follow to make these connections?

Self 2: There is no assurance that change will occur, whichever route is chosen. I decided to take a year and, with other teachers, examine my assumptions about learning. This is not to say that everybody should follow the same path. Many share my concerns but work them out quite differently. Study groups, effective inservicing, and reading and reflecting offer the same possibilities.

Self 1: Can you tell me more about that? The workshops and in-services I go to seem to give the impression that all we have to do is try a few activities, and a new theory of learning will be revealed.

Self 2: I understand what you mean. There doesn't seem to be much thought given to complexity of implementing change. However, connections aren't made immediately. Take my summer-school experience, for example. I worked with a group on a writing project. We were to construct a theme unit for an elementary class. We shared ideas and divided the tasks. Then we worked alone. We drifted together again, shared ideas, and completed the writing. I didn't understand why the writing project went so well till the fall. I discovered then, by writing and responding to writing, that writing is a collaborative activity. During the summer, I had wanted to go off by myself to complete my piece. Because I believed writing to be solitary, I was willing to cut myself off from people who could help.

Self 1: Yes, I can see that you assumed writing was something best done alone; that was evident in your grade-nine essay assignment. The realization that it isn't certainly occurred well after the fact.

Self 2: I think most connections are made that way—we often don't have enough information to make them immediately. Let me relate an incident that demonstrates why writing is different for me now. During the first or second week of classes, we were asked if we considered ourselves writers. What a foolish question, I thought. I'm not a writer. Even though I had published one little piece years ago, I didn't write to publish. Other kinds of writing didn't count. Shortly after, we were invited to write about a "scary incident." Just let it flow without worrying about form or convention, our teacher advised. She called it a freewrite—first time I'd heard that term. Over the next few weeks, we tinkered with the freewrite. In small groups we shared our work, got responses about what readers liked or didn't like and most important what was clear or unclear. My piece changed direction three times and emerged as a narrative about a man and boy in a struggle with a huge fish. The changes I made were sometimes those I wanted to make, but others were prompted by something said in the group or some aspect of another person's writing that I liked and decided to use. That helped me to redefine my concept of "writer." The experience had other effects too. Sharing made me see that writing was the furthest thing from a solitary activity and helped me put my summer experience into perspective.

Self 1: Let me get this straight: you're writing and learning by writing, and you think you are better able to help others because you do. OK so far? You've told me the way kids were writing in the elementary school made you want to know more and that your views of grading, evaluation, convention, and collaboration have changed too. I can understand your beliefs have changed, but how do you know this will work for you?

Self 2: I had that question myself. It wasn't enough to read, reflect, and talk; I needed to see what was happening out there. A friend had invited me to her classroom. She teaches language arts in a junior high school. We had talked about writing many times. I knew writing was an important part of her curriculum. I think it came down to wondering if I could create a community of writers in my classroom based on my own writing experiences. I needed some assurances that it worked for the students too. In my friend's classroom, I saw junior high kids writing about social relationships, sports, and other personal concerns. Many of their pieces were ongoing, having been started in the fall. They were committed to them because the writing was their own. These writers experimented with their writing, especially after a confer-ence. They weren't graded on a final product. Evaluation was based on a continuous consideration of their development as writers and learners. These writers often set their own time limits. And collaboration, wow! They often worked together in small groups on a single piece. Help was always there: from each other, the teacher, style manuals, and dictionaries. There was real writing and real sharing. So I've seen this open-writing context work with junior high students.

Self 1: If everything was working perfectly, there mustn't have been any concerns.

Self 2: There were plenty! There is always uncertainty when you try something new. My friend worried that the kids were finding it difficult to cope with the expectations of two radically different views of learning. When they came to her writing workshop from classes where writing was done only for the teacher, she sensed a certain reluctance, a period when the kids had to realign themselves. She wondered how her students were handling the conflicting messages. I saw evidence in this junior high class of some kids feeling threatened by choice and by being asked to collaborate with others. I can relate to that; I felt that way early in my own course.

Self 1: Being in your friend's classroom helped you see theory in practice, but what if you aren't the language arts teacher when you go back to your school? How will your knowledge of writing help you then?

Self 2: I now see writing as a way of learning rather than as a subject that stands on its own. My friend had to deal with that issue at the beginning of the year. She is responsible for a grade seven health course and wondered what she could do with a body of facts on adolescent social problems. Her view of learning let her offer these kids a way to get the facts. Instead of giving notes and lectures, she turned the course into a writing experience. The facts were embedded in their letters, stories, and plays. Think of it: what better way to deal with the sensitive issues of personal and physical development? Writing can be used across the curriculum. That's why I won't worry if I'm not the English teacher.

Self 1: Well, you seem ready to continue your journey. Do you now have everything you need?

Self 2: Not everything, but writing experiences and the opportunity to learn in a collaborative context have given me a sense of direction. Now I feel prepared to deal with the unexpected. Looking back at the ground I've covered has given me a new sense of adventure.

Creating
a Climate of
Affirmation

Education
Beyond Fear

Marion Anderson

Just the other day, I was substituting in a grade-three classroom. A boy let me know he was present by answering, "We're all here, but we wish we weren't; it's boring."

Until recently, I would have seen this incident simply as a story to relate in the staffroom. From its retelling, some teacher would probably have made a comment such as, "That kid is always making smart remarks—someone should do something about it." The more honest among us would have said or at least thought, "I know exactly how he feels." Then it would have been forgotten.

In one of my graduate classes, however, I have been encouraged to look at these incidents in an entirely new way. They have become a valuable tool, a crystal through which I can examine my assumptions about learning and teaching. I have found they also let me know a great deal about myself. Let me show you where my reflection has led me.

In the incident mentioned at the outset, I responded to the student by saying, "You know, you're not the only one who finds school boring. What do you suggest we do to keep today from being a bore?" I felt good about my reaction, not only because I believe school is boring at times (a good many times), but also because I sensed an immediate kinship with that student. His eyes lit up. He became alert. He saw me as someone who valued his opinion.

My reactions have not always been that positive. I remember times when my kindergarten children would ask me for play time, and I would answer, "Only when your work is finished." I didn't really believe completing pages of carefully formed letters was more important than allowing the children time to interact socially, but that was what my response implied. Or there were the times when I refused to let children play different instruments in the rhythm band.

Why did I refuse when I didn't really believe our concert performance was more important than the children's enthusiasm for playing?

I began noticing that it was not the incidents themselves but my emotional reaction to them that was important. Out of that reaction came a feeling either of satisfaction or dissatisfaction. In situations where I followed my intuition, letting myself respond to the person, I felt confirmed, validated, liberated. When I did what was expected of me and reacted only to the situation, I felt a disloyalty to the students. I wondered why I had continued to respond in ways that clearly did neither me nor the students any good. The more I thought about it, the more I saw that my reluctance to respond on a more personal level was based on fear.

My inability to go with my feelings lay with my fear that I would not be considered a good teacher if I did not meet certain expectations. Students are expected to come to school, listen, and learn the material. Teachers are expected to know this material, teach it and make sure the students understand it.

The control I assumed was made evident to me once during an experience-chart activity with a kindergarten class. After one child had told me what I was to write, I asked, "Are you sure you want to say it like that?" One very vocal little boy answered, "That's how it happened, but we can change it." I had been controlling this activity all along, afraid that if I accepted exactly what the children said, they wouldn't learn good sentence structure. By not accepting their suggestions, I had been telling them they were not good enough.

I was caught between measuring up to the system's expectations of me as a teacher and the realization that nothing unique and creative can come from boredom. This conflict was constantly with me in the classroom. Even when my heart and intuition were telling me I should go beyond my role of teacher, should let the students experience the feeling of success that comes from being in tune with themselves, I was at the same time rationalizing: "The child will lose in the end if he or she can't conform," or "Next year's teacher will expect the children to know a certain amount of material." Looking back, I now have the courage to say I let the system fuel my fears.

The most poignant example of such fear, and the one I find the most difficult to write about, occurred with my son, Jonathan. It's not easy to let go of my fears regarding his marks. He just manages to pass exams. The fact that he began a late French Immersion Programme recently increases my apprehension about good grades. This ongoing conflict came to a climax one evening when he brought home an exam for me to sign that he barely passed. I knew he had spent no time preparing for it. Refusing to listen to any excuse, and out of frustration, I said, "Do you always intend to be a failure?" My fear that my son would get so far behind that he could never catch up; my fear that he would fail the grade; my fear that he would even lose interest in going to school, never get to university; my fear that his teachers would hold me responsible for his low grades; and yes, even my fear that he would hold me responsible in the end if he did fail, were embodied in my remark.

Seeing the tears in his eyes stopped me cold. I suddenly realized that the mark itself was relatively unimportant. Why should it matter to me? Putting my arms around him, I apologized. I wanted to reassure him I loved him for who he is, not for what he does. Later, thinking about what I had done, I realized my fear that he would fail the system (and his being unable to cope with that failure) had prompted all my attempts to get him to study more. Here in the most vivid way was the struggle between what I ultimately believed to be of importance and my apprehension that arose from the expectations I knew the system placed upon my son.

I did not easily set this fear aside. There are times when Jonathan still brings home marks that make me cringe. Times when I have to remind myself he has to find his own way and be supported in that.

Recently, when I visited his school and saw his teacher so caught up with marks that she could relate little else about my son, I felt empathy for her as a colleague. But I also felt sorrow that she is unlikely to take anything from her encounter with Jonathan but a collection of numbers beside his name. She will never know that this child (who couldn't use a telephone book until the day he found a wounded robin and was determined to help it) will always make sense of his world—with or without marks. My desire to have a place in that world is greater than my fear of a "failure" that is defined in so arbitrary a way.

Isn't it our fear that children will fail the system that accounts for many of the practices we institute in the classroom? We give the students worksheets, texts, and packaged knowledge, hoping in the end they will be conditioned enough to ignore any different interpretation they might possibly conceive. We institute many classroom rituals to make students conform. And if they don't conform, we may resort to oppressive language, such as, "Who do you think you are?" or "Didn't I tell you to keep quiet?" All of these responses come from a fear that children will fail the system rather than coming from anything we know about teaching and learning. Only my realization that giving in to this kind of fear shuts me off from what I value most allows me to take steps to overcome it.

Reaching beyond my fear allows me to see each learner as a person with feelings, who through a series of transactions with this world creates his or her reality. What is important to me is not how that reality matches my own but the fact that it is created. When I give positive feedback about that creation to my students, I encourage them to continue to have faith in their attempts to learn. This encouragement not only provides nourishment for them but enriches me as well. I share in their growth. I am also affirmed. The times when I have felt good about my interactions with students, times I have felt I counted, that my role could not be filled by the presence of just another body, were times when I went beyond my role of teacher-assessor to that of teacher-nurturer.

In one of my courses, we were asked to relate a successful learning incident. Although I could think of many, one incident kept returning: I remembered my grandfather teaching me a card game, Auction, when I was about five or six. What I remembered here was not how I learned the game, but the patience and gentleness of this old man. He never insisted I play the way he wanted. He never insisted I think before making a play. He never questioned my intelligence. He let me take the lead. He taught me as we played. I don't remember how he taught me, but I do remember I had no fear I wouldn't learn, and I never sensed that my grandfather thought I wouldn't learn, either. He affirmed me. I felt good about what I was doing and wanted to continue. It seemed natural to learn, and the feeling of openness and caring I sensed from my grandfather was as important to me in learning the game as the practice through playing.

By affirming children, I encourage and demonstrate to them that it's all right to take risks because the results of the risk taking will never be wrong. Freed from the idea of right and wrong, the continual striving to reproduce someone else's meaning (and suffering a guilt when that doesn't happen), they really do become creators. I have realized, at least intuitively and I suspect intellectually, that if I do not affirm children, I negate them, forcing them to be in the same position in which I often found myself. They also know that "there's something more," but they become bound by the fears I impose upon them.

From my reflection and analysis of incidents, I have found that how I behave in the classroom must reflect my belief that feelings play a vital role in learning. Times when I've failed to act on that belief, sacrificed the reality of feeling to authority and rules, were times I gave in to my fear and felt bound in and dissatisfied with my teaching. When I was dissatisfied, I negated children by insisting they accept the information of others rather than create their own insights.

I don't think I will always reach each and every student, but if I approach them in good faith, I have the satisfaction of knowing I've done all I am capable of doing to help them feel valued.

Think of this chapter as an attempt of one teacher to confront a weakness. It was something I needed to write. First, to show myself and others who have experienced or are experiencing the same struggle that we are the makers of our fears, regardless of what prompts us to create them. It is only we who can dismantle them. Second, it is only when we begin dismantling our fears that our inner voice shines through, its light affirming ourselves as well as others.

No fear should ever prevent our demonstrating that.

That First
Year Back

Florence Kanary

When I returned to teaching after eight years' absence, I had many moments of doubt. I remember feeling a bit like the Avis Rent-A-Car ad—always having to try much harder. I wanted to appear as competent as my fellow teachers. Now, looking back, I realize the extra effort forced me to assess some of my assumptions about learning. It turned out I was in for a few surprises when I began to look more closely at what I was doing.

I had been assigned five grade-seven English classes. In each class, the students had been placed in two predetermined levels of the Ginn 360 series. That meant I was expected to use the basal readers along with the corresponding teacher manuals and student workbooks. However, as the weeks passed I became dissatisfied with the program. It was heavy on skills and light on enjoyment. I soon realized that when I was reading with one group, the others always seemed to be eavesdropping instead of completing their assignments on vocabulary, prefixes, suffixes, etc. It suddenly dawned on me—we had much more to gain by working together on stories that interested everyone rather than separating the class into ability-based groups. That was the first of many decisions about learning I made for myself and, small as it was, it was important because once I saw the students enjoying reading, I then had to find out what sort of reading material would interest them. When I introduced books the students liked, I found some of the supposedly slower readers could talk a blue streak on topics that I and others knew nothing about. Our reading now involved everything from motorcycles to space travel. I was flabbergasted. What I learned from the students was that curriculum did need to be relevant.

The long and short of it is this. We stuffed the Ginn 360 books in the cupboard. Instead, I searched for suitable stories and novels from here, there, and everywhere. Students, too, wanted to bring stories and articles to the class, and through this involvement their learning seemed more purposeful to them. Gradually, even the topics for writing were better because we were all talking a lot more. I felt the drudgery diminish—students were happy to come to class to read or to be read to, to talk or to listen, and to write; Overall, we became more relaxed about the curriculum. Often, in the midst of all this hubbub, I thought of old Mr. Wilson, my Educational Methods professor, who always advised "Don't let *them* tell you what to do!" and "Don't crack a smile until January!" His advice seemed so unrealistic as we all learned so much from one another. Besides, I was smiling. It seemed that as the students assumed more responsibility, there was less need for control by me.

Poor Mr. Wilson! What would he have thought about my inviting the county planner for a daylong visit because the students wanted to know more about the new recreational facilities planned for their subdivision? That day, the students had studied and discussed historical and future map projections of their locale. It was a far cry from the skills-based exercises of a few months earlier. It was obvious the students were making sense of things that mattered, and I learned a great deal about the district in which I was teaching.

It was an interesting year! In time we even felt comfortable enough to share writing and reading in groups. I had done some reading on the success of group sharing activities, so I gave it a try. This was more of a struggle for me—I was so concerned with the noise level. I remember how I had been taught—good students were seen, not heard. There were some hairy, scary moments, like the time the school secretary personally delivered a message and commented that she had tried contacting me over the PA, but there had been so much chatter from the students I obviously hadn't heard! The noise level created a real quandary for me. I was so conscious of the teacher next door, from whose class I never heard a peep. Occasionally, she opened the adjoining door, stuck her head in, checked out the situation, and closed the door again! What was I to think? I can chuckle about it now, but then I was intimidated.

Nevertheless, despite the noise, we kept at it. The students were reading enthusiastically, and writing was not as tedious a task as it had been. We still covered the basic conventions like spelling, punctuation, and capitalization, but in a less fragmented way. That's when I again realized students had so much to learn from one another. When a student explained something like period placement to another student, the understanding came more easily. Now, that didn't mean I turned the whole show over to them. I was still teaching, but the lessons were more meaningful because I was allowing for spontaneity. I remember one incident—we had completed a novel, and students in their groups were discussing and sharing their ideas on the similarities and differences of two story settings. They were about to write their first draft, when one student, who to this point had not been particularly successful, rushed up to me and whispered, "May I draw instead, because I can really see it?" Thankfully, I responded, "Of course you may." His eyes lit up, and back he went to the group to begin. The next day, Matt was first to arrive. He toted his drawings, into which he had meticulously incorporated every little detail showing a comparison between the settings. Drawing was a way for him to explain his understanding. Suddenly, Matt and his art work took on a new presence in the class—his artistic effort inspired other displays of creativity. As for me, I again had my eyes opened. Matt had taken responsibility for his own learning, and the outcome had been productive.

Marks, of course, were another concern. I learned quickly that there were still four reporting periods a year, so I was constantly aware of the need to gather marks for the end of the term. I slowly realized that I was going to have to grade the students by using different criteria. I could now see that their willingness to share ideas, to participate in activities, and to undertake editing tasks were important indications of their development.

Taking account of more than correct spelling, grammar, and punctuation seemed fairer, and I saw students profiting in ways I had not seen before. Students like Roy. Roy had come to grade seven with many defeats and few successes as a reader or writer. I sensed he was anxious to please, so I explored a number of avenues to try and engage him. One day, we brainstormed some possible writing topics such as spooky experiences, space frontiers, sports heroes, and rock stars. Roy chose one that interested him, and he immediately sat down to write. Several days later, he shared his story with his group, and it was obvious everyone liked it. Roy beamed and then realized he was going to have to improve it for the next draft. I, too, was impressed with his effort; it was a solid story about the long awaited rain in a desert community. It did, however, contain some blatant deviations from convention. We talked about these, and Roy reworked his piece again. Finally, I realized that if I put any more pressure on him, Roy was likely to back off. Although I knew his story wasn't exceptional, I posted his piece on the writers' bulletin board in the classroom. Roy's reaction upon seeing his writing publicly displayed is one of the teaching hurrahs I will remember forever. Since then, I have heard much discussion about the need to publish only conventionally correct writing, and I understand the arguments advanced. Yet students like Roy need the feeling of accomplishment too. He had put so much of himself into the effort and was so proud of himself, I felt more than justified in rewarding him. Incidents like this showed me clearly that the process itself is important.

I learned a lot that first year back. I was forced into growth by the needs of those students. In a funny way, I can be somewhat grateful to the Ginn 360 program, for it opened my eyes to what students were not responding to. And I learned to turn old Mr. Wilson's advice around. Now I let them tell *me* what to do!

PART FOUR

reflecting

Reflecting, standing back from our experience, is an important part of becoming learning teachers. Each day in the classroom, there are incidents that have the potential to help us learn, both about our students and about ourselves. It isn't always our most recent classroom experiences that help us see ourselves and our teaching with new eyes. We can learn a great deal from past events. There are also insights to be gained in unexpected places. Reflection can be triggered in many different ways. Reading something that catches our attention, finding a drawing in an old scrapbook, coming across a piece of family history, seeing the current mess on the dining room table—all can make us pause and reconsider our world.

Roberta Jones describes how something she's read makes her think differently about her role in the classroom. Her exploration of mistakes that make a difference lead her to realize her students have to learn to recognize their own mistakes if they are to become independent learners.

81

Margot Shutt finds some useful reflection triggered by the mess left over from her family's foray into origami. She uses her son Scott's present achievement to think about his earlier literacy struggles.

Linda Christian shares a lesson from the past. She considers how what she's currently learning about literacy development has helped her understand what one of her first young students was trying to tell her.

Nancy Anthony makes an unexpected connection while wallpapering her son's bedroom. The family growth chart on his wall raises some critical questions for her about how we evaluate and grade students.

Looking for
Mistakes That Make
a Difference
Roberta Jones

"You put your shirt on backwards."
"Your coat is not hung up."
"You left toys in the driveway."
"Your socks don't match."
"You forgot your lunch."

Right from the beginning, children are informed about their mistakes. Either they recognize these mistakes for themselves or some kind soul points them out. As we get older we may shed the mistakes of our youth, but we still make mistakes, in one form or another. Some of my more memorable mistakes have included leaving kleenex in my pants pockets, not covering up the frogs when cleaning their tank, and not cooking sausages long enough. I know these are mistakes because of their consequences: my clothes have been covered with white lint when they come out of the washer, I have had to chase slippery frogs all over the basement, and my husband has felt sick after supper.

Frank Smith (1983) contends that there are two kinds of mistakes: those that make a difference and those that don't. He argues that those that do make a difference are evident, and we learn from them. You can guess what kind of mistakes mine are, but what about the mistakes with which I began? Do they make a difference? To whom do they make a difference?

Generally, mistakes are treated as something bad in school: classmates snicker, teachers frown, and parents are embarrassed. Mistakes are something to be avoided. Smith argues, however, that mistakes are far from being a dead end. In most cases they can offer a beginning, new directions, or options to explore. Those mistakes that make a difference usually are very evident because of their consequences. We learn from these mistakes; they are helpful.

83

Teachers and students need to be able to recognize mistakes for what they are—a learning opportunity. Let me share a few mistakes that have helped me learn about teaching.

Tommy, usually an adept writer, was fidgeting and listless during journal writing one day. I asked him, "Aren't you writing today?" He paused for a moment and then began moving his pen across the paper. During lunch, as I read through the journals, Tommy's entry made me choke on my tuna fish sandwich. "No, Mrs. Jones I am not writing anything today." I had mistaken Tommy's physical act of writing as an indication that he was doing fine. Instead of pulling up a chair and talking with him about his difficulties, I merely asked a useless question, a question that caused Tommy to answer in a flippant way. Did I help him write? No, I helped him decide not to write that day. My mistake. This mistake, in fact, helped me look at my conferencing techniques as I went from child to child. I learned to let the children show me how I might be of help to them.

Then there was five-year-old Sarah, so upset one day that she had a tantrum in the classroom. However, instead of comforting her, I bent down and demanded an explanation. Sarah left teeth marks. With that, all of our anger dissolved and we sat on the floor to discuss the problem. It amounted to very little—Sarah had lost her snack. We solved it with a quick search of the classroom. From this mistake, I learned to react to the problem itself rather than to the emotion of the moment.

I also remember the day I left the painting easel too close to the reading corner. It didn't take long before paint-splattered books had my attention. I moved the easel to the back of the classroom.

But what about mistakes that don't make a difference? During March break I decided to paint my bathroom. My daughter was concerned about people touching the freshly painted walls, so she tacked a sign to the door, "WAT PAT." Combined with the smell of the paint and Samantha's sign, it was obvious where not to touch the walls. The spelling mistakes in the sign did not make a difference.

There was also the occasion when a student and I were reading a book about keeping zoo animals as pets. Gary read, "But he was too long," instead of, "But he was too tall." I questioned his use of *long*. Did *long* start with *T*? He replied, "What difference does it make? We know they both mean that the giraffe is too big to keep." I had to agree; his mistake did not make a difference to the meaning of the story. I saved the lesson about the difference between long and tall for another day. Gary wanted to get on with his story, so I let him.

No matter how we look at it, there are always going to be mistakes. The decision I, as teacher, have to make is how to react to these mistakes. Tom Romano (1987) says it succinctly, "Am I nurturing children as learners—or am I highlighting mistakes for the purpose of evaluation—rather than learning?"

The children are quick to understand my standpoint on this issue. If I make all the decisions about what is right and what is wrong, if I give them the answers, if I dictate the usage of materials, and if

I indiscriminately correct all mistakes, then I become evaluator. But if I give the children some freedom to discover which mistakes make a difference and work with them to learn from these mistakes, then I am a nurturer.

Four-year-old Alison was busy typing a story on the computer. She called to me and said, "How do I make this part speak?" I pulled up a chair and showed her how to enclose her dialogue between quotation marks.

Wos o pon a tim ther wos a lad full of fobs wun day the fobs sed "Wi is twig ows hang ord rharsis"
thn wun day twig cam and tuk ol ther fud
the end

Translation

Once upon a time there was a land full of fobs. One day the fobs said, "Why is Tweeg always hanging around our houses?"
Then one day Tweeg came and took all their food.
The end.

In the past year, I have watched Alison learn to read and write by just doing that—reading and writing. She takes control and, when she gets stuck, she asks for help. I listen to her and respond to her questions. In the case of her question about the quotation marks, I merely showed her how to use this punctuation so she could get on with the task at hand—writing. I did not correct her functional spelling. But I do notice that Alison does come to me to help her correct spelling mistakes if she can't read back what she has composed.

Don't think finding those mistakes that make a difference is an easy task. There are many times when they really only make a difference to me and not to the learner. It is at this point that I have to stop and ask myself, "Who does the mistake make a difference to?" As a teacher, I know I can't possibly correct all the mistakes my children and I make, so why not just worry about those that make a difference to the learner? Although I may be comfortable doing that, others may not be. Administrators, teachers, and parents all try to influence how I teach. They may even fog my perception of what may really make a difference to the learners in my classroom. However, in the end I have to decide what really makes a difference. . . . and so do my students.

But I Don't Think So

The teacher says I have to print with a pencil and color with crayons.
But colors help me write funny stories.

The teacher says I have to work quietly and not disturb anyone.
But Sarah knows about my pet frog, and she can help me remember.

The teacher says I have to be finished in ten minutes.
But my hand is tired, and I want to think about my spaceship now.

The teacher says I have to read at my desk.
But I am more comfortable on the floor.

The teacher says I have to take my time and work neatly.
But I always forget what I want to say when I write slowly.

The teacher says I have to learn how to spell alligator.
But I really want to learn how to spell dinosaur names so I can
edit my story.

The teacher says she knows best.
But I don't think so.

References

Romano, Tom. 1987. *Clearing the Way.* Portsmouth, NH:
Heinemann.
Smith, Frank. 1983. *Essays Into Literacy.* Portsmouth, NH:
Heinemann.

Side by Side
Margot Shutt

Bright sunshine beamed through the window and focused my attention on the bits of colored paper that covered the dining room table and spilled over onto the floor. Making the delicate yellow, green, red, and blue origami flowers and animals had proved to be a challenge. I find myself smiling as I recall the rising excitement in my sons' voices as we achieved our first success; then there was the time I was ready to admit defeat, only to be encouraged and supported by the boys; and still again, the time I was able to help them succeed with the difficult paper-folding project they had chosen. The learning together was what was special. But it hasn't always been this way. Learning hasn't always been happy in our house.

I remember my first efforts to help my younger son, Scott, learn to read. We sat at the table together. The situation was tense, the book between us, dividing us. "But Scott, you've got to try! Sound it out. What is the first letter?" A mumbled response. I continued. "What does it sound like?" A mumble again. I persisted and moved on to the middle part of the word. My frustration built up. "What's wrong with my child? Why can't he read?" I'd ask myself. It didn't occur to me that maybe I was the one at fault, that perhaps my efforts were harming rather than helping. I had learned to read this way; why couldn't Scott?

Wasn't he trying? Wasn't he paying attention? That wasn't the Scott I knew. He seemed to be refusing to learn, so I made a visit to his teacher to find out what was going on.

It was difficult to be honest in our conversation. For a moment, I had felt tempted to blame the teacher. But how could I do that and still ask for help? She shared a lot of new ideas about reading with me. I was skeptical, to say the least. Yet at the back of my mind, I could see Scott's hand tightly clenched as he tried to read for me.

Although I had ignored this sign of his discomfort, that clenched fist became significant as the teacher continued to reveal her reading strategies in Scott's class. And they seemed to connect with the boy who loved to draw or to make models, the one who would spend hours attempting to do it just right. Yes, it was worth a try. I must admit that it was worth more than that. I was desperate! Too much was at stake. I was prepared to try almost anything.

The expression "old ways die hard" unfortunately proved true. It wasn't easy for me to change. From the moment the teacher described what she was doing, I had found myself resisting and, at times, balking at her suggestions. I often reverted to old ways. However, what occurred was an evolution, rather than a sudden dramatic change.

In the Beginning ... The teacher shared some of her impressions of Scott with me. One I particularly remember. "Are you and your Mum reading these library books?" she asked Scott one day on their return journey from the library. He nodded his head; that was the end of their conversation. Imagine my embarrassment as his teacher shared the incident, and I had to admit I hadn't seen the library books. Scott had been carrying books home, yet he spent no time looking at them. It was obvious to her that he wanted to look like a reader, to be a reader, but that he didn't think he could. She suggested involving Scott in some reading with a personal purpose, some reading connected to something he wanted to do or make.

I spent considerable time trying to come up with an idea before I approached Scott. The teacher had emphasized that it had to be something that Scott would like to do, not something I thought would be good for him. Also, it would do no good if I forced the issue. I found myself analyzing his favorite activities for possibilities. I finally made a choice: cooking. Scott loved to help out in the kitchen. I broached the idea very casually while we were in the local bookstore one day. I was standing in front of a rack of cookbooks. "Scott, look at this," I said, and pointed to the shelf. He fell for it! He chose a microwave cookbook, and we promptly returned home to try his first recipe. I won't say it was easy. Not all his results were successful, but we did read together. And it was fun! In retrospect, the reading was incidental. The strong purpose had been crucial. So was the time we spent together.

The teacher also emphasized the need to be reading stories together at home. This really upset me. With good reason, I felt—we had been reading to Scott for a long time. But the teacher said he needed control over this reading. In my defense, I talked about our visits to the library, and how I helped Scott to choose his books. But a closer analysis revealed that I had held the upper hand as I had pushed particular books at him—ones I thought he might like, not necessarily the ones he would have chosen himself. So I learned to relinquish the control. It really wasn't so hard. What surprised me was that Scott selected some good books! And if he didn't like the ones he did bring home, well, we just didn't read them a second time. And because he so enjoyed choosing the books, he would push to visit the library more often. So the library visits became a regular activity, not the sporadic trips they once had been.

In addition, we changed our story-reading routine. Reading together at bedtime had often suffered in our busy household. Now, we read stories just after the dinner chores were done, which was a more relaxed time in the evening. It became a sharing time, one during which Scott and I would read together. I was able to enjoy our time together without having to hurry Scott to bed. And I found I was becoming less anxious about Scott and his reading.

I must emphasize that these changes did not occur overnight. I had many conversations with Scott's teacher. We spent a lot of time talking about predictable books. I didn't understand how a child could learn to read from them. Oh, I'd heard children recite sections of a predictable book. "Obviously memorized," had been my reaction. I had no notion of how a child could read without deciphering letters and words.

But the teacher was able to convince me otherwise. She asked me to read a sentence that was incomplete. She wrote "The birthday cake had nine————. I automatically supplied the word *candles*. "Yes," she said. "And that's how these books work. They contain familiar actions that children know and understand. Children are able to develop an ability to predict, that is, guess words and actions, from the context of the story. They move beyond the memorization stage in their efforts to make sense of the story. Cues for words and actions are also found in the pictures. Yes, it would have been even easier for me to guess the word *candles* if the teacher had drawn a birthday cake with candles on top.

Things had become a little clearer to me, but I still didn't understand how children learn words and letters. She explained it as a process where children first predict and use picture cues. Then they learn to focus on print cues as they progress. Once they realize the print contains the message, they begin to recognize individual letters and words. Then, she said, they're on their way to independent reading. Predictable books, apparently, allow children to read and develop confidence before the print cue sources are well developed.

So we added predictable books to our library selections. And Scott did all the things the teacher said he would. He joined in as I read. He jumped ahead of me. He guessed what was on the next page. He was even able to predict word endings. Sometimes he would join in before we completed a first reading; sometimes it would not be until a second or third. I began to think maybe there was something to this after all.

The teacher had also insisted I not correct Scott as he began to read independently. Why? I wondered. I thought I would just be helping him with the words. No, what I would actually be doing was confusing him in his efforts to predict or to make sense of the print. If he was reading for meaning and it made sense, he would read on. If it didn't, he would reread to attempt to make sense. But I also wondered about words he did not know. Should I tell him, or let him guess? I must admit I often supplied missing words only to later discover that Scott had come to rely on me and wouldn't attempt to figure them out himself. I must also admit that this was the most difficult time for me. I discovered little tricks like reading softly with him, quietly supplying words when necessary and taking turns when we read. *And it worked!*

Scott's confidence grew. Gone were the tightly clenched fists and the mumbled words, replaced by a smiling boy. I remember the day it hit me that Scott could read. One evening, Scott and I sat comfortably on the sofa. "Hey, Mum, listen to this," Scott said as he showed me a book from the school library. "Is this ever neat." And he began to read in a happy, clear voice. He sped along. Whoops, he missed a word. The sentence didn't make sense, and back he went to try again. Then he hit a word he couldn't figure out, so he stumbled but he quickly moved on. I was relaxed. I knew he would ask me if he needed my help. Not all that long ago, I would have been critically looking for what was wrong. Now, at last, I was able to promote his taking risks, his reading to make sense.

We learned together. The book no longer divided us. Rather, it joined us in our efforts. I came to understand how choice and interest play such an important part in learning to read. I recall how Scott's first choices of Garfield and Heathcliff books frustrated me. I even learned to accept his desire to read the same book over and over again. I realized the familiarity was helping him develop confidence. He soon moved on to other kinds of reading.

I used to hate the days Scott would come home from school with order forms from book clubs. I'm afraid it was my visions of the unread books on his shelf that prompted my comments. "But Scott, do you really think you want this one? Will you read it?" Since the response was inevitably "yes," I'd always agree to purchase one or two. Looking back, I'm certain Scott sensed my distrust. As he began to feel good about himself and his beginning success in reading, I noticed our attitudes changed. We came to enjoy the days when the order forms came home, and we would mull over the choices together.

We moved on in other ways too. I became more than a supporter. We began to read science and geography books. I became as excited as Scott did when we learned new geowhiz facts from the latest National Geographic Children's book. The mounds of origami designs also bear witness to our mutual learning. My desire to help Scott learn to read turned into something unexpectedly worthwhile. I stopped telling my child what and how to read. Reading became something we shared as we learned together.

We even attempted to write notes to one another. The teacher had talked about writing and how it could help reading. Now, I knew Scott was writing at school; he would sometimes share his writing with me. So I wrote him a message, asking a question, and left it on his bedroom door. Pleased to receive it, Scott promptly replied. We continued in this manner for a number of days, until I discovered that my notes were being left unanswered. Imagine my surprise when I returned home from evening class three months later to discover a note on the door from Scott. It said, "Hi, Mum, I had a really good day. Swimming was okay. Dad got me new sneakers. Will you spray them tonight? Love, Scott." Knowing I would not be home till long past his bedtime, he had had a purpose for writing.

Scott has seen the rest of the family writing this year.

Consequently, he has also decided to write at home. I've shared my writing with him, asking for his opinions and suggestions, and he in turn has shared his writing with me. We're learning here too. Where once I might have been critical of improper sentences, unpunctuated work, and wrong spelling, I now concentrate on the meaning, the message. I tried hard to become a supportive parent and not repeat the mistake I had made with beginning reading. The results have paid off. Because I did not criticize his spelling mistakes or his improper sentences, Scott learned to take risks that broadened his efforts and his success. Furthermore, he began to learn how to handle the surface features of writing in the process.

I believe that Scott became a reader and a writer because he learned how exciting it could be for him. He had wanted to read and write like the rest of the family, but we hadn't been able to make him feel he could be a part of it. The trusting and supportive relationship we slowly built together allowed him to take the risk, to try and learn with us.

Scott has independently extended his reading and writing, although we still share together. Lately, I have noticed he is spending considerable time writing to a cousin. He also makes the time to read independently. He favors the last half hour before lights-out to reread his old favorites and to begin new books. I often hear him say, "Mum, just let me finish this chapter," or "Mum, only two pages more." I've even seen the flashlight flick off quickly, long after bedtime. And his latest activity is getting up to read first thing in the morning.

Scott and I still talk about some of the things we first did and the struggles we had. One day, I asked him how he would help a friend learn to read. His response, with a twinkle in his eye, was "Read. Read lots of books, books that he likes."

What Denise
Tried to Show Me
Linda Christian

Unlike my grandmother, who stored her memories in her head, my memories are stored in my scrapbooks. Newspaper clippings and the occasional drawing or note from a student transport me to an earlier time in my life.

Every time I come across Denise's drawing of me getting married, seventeen years are erased. I am back in that classroom with forty-five empty desks, waiting for the children I have never met. I feel so alone—part of me dreading the start of school, part of me excited about meeting my first class.

The bell rings, the door bursts open, and I am knee deep in seven-year-olds. The chaos subsides and before I know it, someone is tugging at my skirt. Huge brown eyes stare up at me. Later, I would know that this was Denise, but for now I concentrate on what she is trying to tell me. "Miss, in grade two we don't need two spaces to print. Next time when you write on the board, you can use one space."

How could I have known the difference? I had trained to teach high school. This was the first time I had set foot in a primary classroom. Things had changed a lot since I had been in grade two.

Days became weeks, and with the help of my program guides I felt more secure about teaching. I grew to love the children's spontaneity and eagerness. Take, for example, the day Denise arrived with a copy of *Grimms' Fairy Tales* to share with the rest of us. I close my eyes and see her lugging the huge shopping bag into the classroom. The weight of her hidden treasure forces her to drag the bag across the floor. Hearing the shuffling sound and cries from the other children, I put my planbook aside. It is like Christmas morning as we guess what might be in her bag. Finally, we ask Denise to show us. She removes the copy of *Grimms' Fairy Tales* slowly. Although we can now understand why the package has been

93

so heavy, we can't anticipate her other surprise. She finds a comfortable place to sit and invites us to listen to her read her favorite story, "Hansel and Grethel."

Denise's bringing her book and sharing her favorite story started a chain reaction in the classroom. More shopping bags appeared as children clamored to read at story time. So many children were wanting to read that we had to divide into groups so everyone could have a turn sharing his or her favorite book.

Denise loved this story sharing. She would sit spellbound as she listened to me or the other children read. One day, as I was nearing the end of *Charlotte's Web*, the bell rang. Before I could put the book down, Denise rushed up to me to ask if she could have the book. She wanted to take it home to finish. She just couldn't wait to hear the ending. I smiled to myself, recalling the struggle I'd had persuading Denise to follow along as other children read orally in class. She never knew where to begin when it was her turn to read, for she was always reading ahead.

I tried sitting beside Denise to keep her on track as other children took turns reading. This worked for a while, but the minute I moved away, she became so involved in the story that she was oblivious to anything happening around her.

I don't think she read ahead to annoy me. She couldn't stop herself. Time after time, I had to ask her to put her storybooks away because she had reading workbook exercises to do. How she despised those worksheets! When she ran out of time in school, I made her complete her work at home. I felt that somehow I had to help her understand the importance of those exercises. After all, how was she ever going to learn how to read if she didn't complete the work in the basal reading program?

I believed Denise was too young to understand why I kept after her to finish her work. But since I thought I knew what was best for her, I learned to keep a close watch on her in class. She was my class dreamer, always in a world of her own. This was especially true when I introduced new concepts to the class. When I saw the faraway look in Denise's eyes, I often asked her a question to draw her back to the task at hand.

Sometimes I would ask Denise a question just to see what she would say. There was the day I spent my lunch hour carefully drawing an ice-cream sundae on the blackboard. I had tried so hard to make it look real—right down to the pink, white, and brown chalk neapolitan ice cream. I had no way of knowing what my students would think, but I certainly didn't expect Denise's reaction. She was so engrossed in one of her books while other members of the class were talking about their favorite kinds of ice cream that she was taken off guard when I asked her to tell me what I had drawn on the board. She studied the picture carefully before she timidly replied, "Is it a spin top, Miss?" When the laughter subsided, Denise told us the colors of the ice cream and shape of the sundae dish reminded her of her little brother's spin top. As we looked at my drawing more closely, we could see what Denise meant.

After this incident, children sought Denise's advice when they had difficulty getting their pictures to look the way they wanted them.

Soon they realized Denise's drawing ability came from lots of practice. Her desk was covered with scraps of paper, and when she had free time she drew pictures. After she had been flower girl at her aunt's wedding, all her pictures were related to weddings. I was touched when she left a picture of me as a bride on my desk. I wrote her a note to thank her for her picture and told her I would put it away in a safe place.

My reply to Denise's picture was the start of a private correspondence between us. Over time her notes grew longer, and I noticed that even though she did not always use conventional spelling, I had no difficulty reading what she wrote. She often spent recess time writing and continued when she was supposed to complete exercises. Usually, I tried to coax her along, to engage her in the school work, but some days my patience would run thin. In a stern voice I'd tell her that if she didn't learn how to spell, she'd never know how to write. My constant reminder had no effect on Denise. Too often during writing class, she had seen me running around (like a chicken with her head cut off), spelling words the children needed in their writing. It was utter chaos trying to answer the forest of hands demanding my attention. By the end of writing class, I would be exhausted. The resulting headache was so intense that it would take me three or four weeks to regain the courage to let the children write again.

Denise found it impossible to wait for me to recover from the chaos of our writing classes. When she couldn't steal time away from her work, she wrote at home. The fruits of her labor were left inconspicuously on my desk.

Searching for Denise's notes became part of my daily ritual. When June rolled around, I realized I didn't want the school year to end. There was no way I could have prepared myself for the last day. Denise stood in the doorway of the classroom, tears flowing down her face, adamant that she wasn't leaving. My heart went out to her, and I could no longer hold back the tears that welled inside me. I picked her up, the same way a parent would console a child, and together we walked down the steps to the front of the school where her dad was waiting.

Denise, as I promised, I did put your picture away for safekeeping. It is only now that I understand what you were trying to show me. It took me seventeen years to understand what you knew then: we learn to read by reading and we learn to write by reading and writing.

Celebrating Growth

Nancy Anthony

I started to wallpaper my son's room last August. I wanted to complete the job while I had the time. I didn't finish. I papered around the room to the final wall and then stopped. I couldn't cover the next space. It had my children's growth chart on it—their height, the date, and sometimes their weight marked in pencil and pen right on the paint.

We're still using this, I thought. Only the other day, Steven dragged me in here to measure him. And afterwards, we had looked over his various other entries—his height at ten, his fastest growing period, where he passed me, his father, and his sister. A few friends had also been measured. Their ages were recorded too. This chart was a positive, happy documentation of my children's growth, a piece of family history. I couldn't bury it.

Then I thought about the children's school report cards. Did they evoke the same nostalgic feelings? No, they didn't, because they weren't all success stories. The chart on the wall records only advancement. It has no regression. Nobody shrinks. But report cards often show a decline. For example, when Steven received an eighty in math the first term and a fifty-five the second, red lights flashed! He was losing ground, it said. But he surely didn't know less, even though his report card implied that he did.

A school report should be a celebration of children's learning, just as the growth chart celebrates how much they've grown. In addition, the growth chart isn't accompanied by descriptions of some ideal child used for comparing children's growth, inch by inch. School report cards are, though. In school, children are constantly being measured against some hypothetical standard. Furthermore, a glance at the growth chart shows that children have had different growth patterns. School report cards, however, imply that everyone's growth should look the same.

How might we change report cards so they celebrate our children's growth? Do you suppose we might change what they're called? How about using "growth chart?" Imagine hearing, "Steven, did you grow today? Let's see what you've learned." What would be on the charts? Could there be a place for students to record the titles of books they've read, books they've written, and a list of conventional spelling they've used this term? This information would be easily accessible to students, since they would be collecting it regularly themselves throughout the term. Then they could be responsible for filling out a portion of their own growth charts to take home.

There could also be a summary of skills and strategies the teacher has observed students using, what they can do independently and what they have been able to accomplish with some support. The teacher could document each student's progress and add it to the growth chart at reporting time.

Growth charts such as these would show what students can do— not what they can't. It would show periods of rapid growth, some smaller gains, some plateaus, but never regression. Children do not regress in their learning. They are constantly learning new things. The school report card should be a positive document for every child, something everyone can be proud of. Just like the family growth chart.

PART FIVE

coping with conflict

An important aspect of exploring our assumptions about teaching is coming to terms with the conflicts that arise. As a teacher commented to me recently, "we live in multiple realities." By that, she meant we often see the classroom in fragmented ways. We hold one set of beliefs for what we do in reading, another for writing. We think about mathematics and science with yet other assumptions. Recognizing that we are sending students contradictory messages forces us to begin changing.

Brian MacDonald explores some inconsistencies between his espoused theories and his instructional practices that helped him think about his teaching as a whole differently.

In addition to coming to terms with our personally conflicting theoretical views, becoming a learner-directed teacher creates other kinds of conflict. As our teaching changes, we affect others—our students, their parents, other teachers, principals, supervisors—all are touched by what we do in our classrooms. Conflicts arising from people's different perceptions of what teaching should be like are to be expected. However, resolving these conflicts isn't always easy.

"Dear Mrs. Gillon" is a fictional account based on an incident experienced by Jan Gillin. In it, Jan reveals the conflicts encountered by a classroom teacher when she tries to implement a more open, interpretive classroom in a largely trans-mission context.

Why Didn't This Chicken Cross the Road?

Brian MacDonald

The educational community seems to be divided into two camps—
those who believe in a holistic approach to educational practice
and those who hold more traditional teaching views. More traditional
teachers tend to see their role in the classroom as the providers of
knowledge, a knowledge the students are expected to absorb and
recall on demand. Holistic teachers, however, do not view the
educational process as a one-way transmission of information;
instead, they hold a transactional view of teaching. From a
transactional perspective, both teachers and students are seen as
sharing a journey that allows for unexpected learning for everyone,
including the teachers. Between these two positions stretches a
broad continuum of educational practice, a sort of "no man's land"
where as educators, we find ourselves torn between conflicting
teaching theories.

No one wants to inhabit no man's land, and up to a few months
ago, I felt I was safely lodged in the holistic camp. I had even
ordered my HOLISTIC TEACHER sweatshirt, certain of my membership.
It was from this position of safety that doubts began to assail me.

It was just a few small things at first, but they were enough to
make me question the holistic label I had granted myself. I was
beginning to see the gap between my stated educational beliefs and
my actual classroom practice. There was, for example, the time I
brought the writing workbook to class and assigned exercises. I
cringe when I think of that one, for the work involved drilling writing
skills as ends in themselves. The workbook focused on correcting
openings, closings, run-on sentences, and ambiguous meanings. At
best, it might produce better editors. But help students become
better writers? Not likely. For at no time was any writing ever handled
as a whole entity. My students could actually finish all this "busy
work" and still not have developed a complete paragraph.

Then there was the time I was teaching the novel *Underground to Canada*, a story about fugitive slaves in the mid-nineteenth century. At one point I gave my students a content-based test that included a map of the slaves' route on their journey northward. I asked the students to identify particular locations and discuss the significance of each. Later, I asked myself whether a knowledge of southern geography was what I truly wanted my students to take away from the novel. A sense of outrage over the conditions of slavery or identification with the young characters was far more important than the location of the plantations. My failure to question my instruction in light of my professed beliefs allowed such glaring inconsistencies to exist.

These incidents shook me, but did not substantially alter my belief that I was in fact a holistic teacher. It took the journal-writing experience to do that. Journal writing was one of the main elements I envisioned in my holistic-writing classroom. First, I reviewed the literature on journal writing, paying particular attention to any pieces that dealt with the successful classroom startup. Then, I discussed the process with a colleague whose students produced excellent journal work. Armed with all this information, I typed a whiz-bang introductory package for my students and launched the enterprise on a bright Monday morning. Things got off to a good start—after all, there's nothing like a little hoopla to wake students up. I stood before my classes like a snake oil salesman and told them that the journal would make them into better writers, expand their horizons, and generally cure anything that ailed them. My selective memory had conveniently forgotten the last course I had taken, where journal writing had been mandatory. It was a type of writing I soon came to despise, and I had used a number of dodges to avoid and generally subvert the task. But such things would never happen in my class. I was confident my students would create great journals. After all, that was what whole language was about, and I was a whole language teacher.

Well, things didn't go exactly as planned. It soon became obvious that, despite my instructions to the contrary, my young writers considered the journals to be a sort of diary-writing activity. The entries were boring, both for the students and for me. They lacked the energy so evident in most of their other manuscripts. Almost everyone had the required minimum completed by month's end. Everyone, that is, except me. I was one of the backsliders. Sometimes I wrote with the classes, but student questions, PA interruptions, and the like often kept me from finishing my entries. What I had written, I shared with my students, but there wasn't a lot to share. It also took longer than expected to get the journals back in their hands. My planned forty-eight hour turnaround time dissolved in the face of a journal avalanche of nine hundred entries. The journal writing limped along throughout the year, but something was seriously wrong. A small number of students showed improvement. Most, however, were stuck in a sort of writer's limbo. I had initiated journal writing, expecting great things; yet only a handful of individuals experienced significant growth as writers.

The next summer, I enrolled in a writing class and had the

opportunity to reflect on the experience. Yes, I had stressed the importance of journal writing; yes, I had written encouraging comments; and yes again, I had tried to have the students think of themselves as writers. My teaching reflected most of the conventions mentioned in the literature, so what had gone wrong? Gradually, I realized that I had not understood the real purpose of the journals, nor had I communicated to my students the sense of journal writing as dialogue. This should have been the foundation of my teaching. In the headlong rush to "get the job done," I had failed to realize that the only job that needed doing was to create an atmosphere where writing was meaningful. I had perceived the journals as just another assignment to be completed by my students. They read the agenda correctly and responded accordingly. The time, effort, and resources poured into this activity had not resulted in their becoming more proficient writers. At this point in time, the holistic educator title seemed to ring hollow.

This feeling was emphasized by the infamous newspaper assignment. I had never granted the students real freedom as writers, for I had dominated the writing agenda with *my* ideas. One of my not-so-original brainstorms was to have the students create their own newspaper. Like most writing projects presented to the class, I had organized it as an event. On my desk, I had a list of possible sections we might include in the paper. There was a rough timeline for the due dates, editing, photocopying, stapling, and distribution. As far as I was concerned, everything was in place. We began by brainstorming what the class felt should be included in the paper. I was certain their list would affirm the one I had already in mind.

However, from the start, they saw potential I had failed to envision in this paper. They suggested newspaper columns I had not dreamed of: gossip columns, personalized horoscopes, a rock video rating, and, of course, fashion advice for both "preps" and "headbangers." My staid suggestions for book reviews and "at the movies" columns were met with a less-than-enthusiastic response. Oh, they did get written, but I knew in my heart that the students were only including these elements to humor me, for this was their paper and they had set its tone. They wrote the articles, edited them, made legible copies, did the photocopying, and distributed the finished product. The general grumblings over a technical delay showed their eagerness to see their writing in all its splendor. The newspaper was a success, because the students had the good sense to take it out of my hands and into their own. They had made the project a meaningful activity, and I realized just how much could be accomplished when my students were granted the freedom to make decisions as writers.

I was beginning to consider the hard truth. I had not truly committed myself to a holistic teaching perspective, and yet I wasn't a traditional transmission teacher either. I was exactly where I didn't want to be—squarely in the middle of the road. As uncomfortable as this realization is, it had some advantages. For one, I could no longer delude myself about being a holistic teacher. The old transmission-based instructor who stood in the front of his or her classroom had been banished, but in his or her stead was a sort of hybrid. I was at times a holistic educator, yet I often did business from the same old stand. This created confusion for my students, for they were confronted with a teacher who espoused one set of educational beliefs and yet created situations that elicited the usual memorize-and-regurgitate strategies. Like the pirates of old, I'd been flying false colors, and the deception, unintentional though it may have been, undermined my credibility in their eyes.

How did I end up in this position? The answer is simple. When I climbed on board the whole language bandwagon, I didn't understand the nature of the journey. At the time, it appeared to be a new method of teaching; only later did I realize that the successful implementation of a holistic perspective necessitated a change in the way I viewed my teaching world. In the rush to "do" whole language, I merely altered my existing teaching practices, not my beliefs. Without that change in educational philosophy, any holistic methods I employed would always fall short of my expectations. Despite my claims to the contrary, the learning situations and demonstrations existing in my classroom speak clearly about my adherence to old beliefs about learning.

My failure to approach teaching situations from a truly holistic perspective has a high price. My students miss learning opportunities, and I could lose rewarding teaching experiences. Like the time I learned about Murphy's one-eyed dog. A fellow teacher extended me the invitation to help her with a writing project she wanted to begin with one of her resource groups. The project involved having some students write and produce their own radio program. When the two of us sat down to brainstorm the idea, I immediately began listing the sort of things I thought the students should include in their writing. The words *Ads/News/Weather* had appeared on the top of the paper, when I began to actually hear what she was saying about allowing the students to find their own direction. Visions of the newspaper experience raced through my mind, and I realized that I had been reverting to form. The old, directive-giving educator had surfaced, but this time I stopped him short.

A few days later, after a visit to a radio station, we sat down with the children. As they chatted about what they thought belonged on the air, Murphy, a shy diminutive boy who had been very quiet, told of his one-eyed dog. That dog, and the story of how he lost his eye, captured everyone's interest. It became a part of their radio broadcast. Imagine if I had come to this meeting with my preconceived list of topics. Murphy might never have had the chance to discuss his handicapped pet, and a prime motivation for his writing would have been lost.

There was a time when I would not have questioned my actions or beliefs. Review and reassessment are now the order of the day. I have changed as an educator, and the way I view my role in the educational process has been transformed. The ringmaster who announced each academic performance has gone, and in his place is a guide, someone who works harder to lead students over territory both familiar and unexplored. My practice has finally caught up with my beliefs. This chicken *has* finally crossed the road.

18

"Dear Mrs. Gillon"
Jan Gillin

dear Mrs. Gillon.

dear MrsGillin I think its fun to write a letter in a sircl. do you lik it? from Mary Catherine

P.S. Mary C. has a dental appointment next Tues. at 3 pm. I'll be there to pik her up at reless. -M.

Dear Mrs Gillin,
This is a quick note to say how much I appreciate your enthusiasm with Mary C's writing. Her father and I are delighted to see her so eager to write again after the struggles she had with a "perfectionist" last year in grade two at our other school.
Sincerely,
Martha Grant.

Sept 28, 1988.

Dear Mrs. Grant,
Thanks so much for your positive comments about Mary Catherine's writing.
She can't help but go far with so many encouraging people around her!
Sincerely,
Jan Gillin

P.S. We'd love to have you come early and see some of our dragon research. See if you can fit us in, okay?

Deer Mrs. Gilion
    I lik riting
stores with you.
I hav a nyew
chptr.

                    from
                       Shannon

chaptr. 2
One day my dad And me fickesed
tle motter on an old truck.it
was raroly fun After that we
had supper. Tomollow I will go
to Straferd to Play hokey.

            Shannon

Oct 12, 1998.

Dear Shannon's
teacher,

Yesterday my son
Shannon he brought home
this work and I
want to no how
come he say you
dont care about this
spelling and if that's
true then I want to
come and see you
because see you
he's got to learn how
to spell.
Are you a teacher
or what?
Sincerly
Mrs. Curtis

Dear Mrs. Gillon
When can I
go and show Mr.
Armstrag my car
story?
From
Shannon.

October 14th,
1988.

Dear Mrs. Curtis,
Thank you for your letter.
It arrived safely with Shannon,
and I wanted to reply to your
concern about his spelling.
Shannon has some really
wonderful story ideas – especially
about his father's service
station and repair work! He
certainly knows more about the
inside of a car than I do!
In my classroom, story
ideas are written down each day
and sometimes the children read
their work to me and to their
classmates. We spend a great deal
of time talking about what
we later write about, and it is
by talking that our ideas become
clearer.
The work that Shannon brought
home is something he has been
really excited about. He has
decided to put together a
collection of stories about his
father's service station and
he is working hard to organize
his ideas.
Right now I am not
concerned with Shannon's
spelling in his work. It is
more important that he
collect and write down all
the information that he needs.
Correct spelling is something
we'll worry about later, when
he is ready to publish his
writing for others to read.
I would really like to
have you come and experience
our classroom. Your questions
and concerns are often easily
answered when you see your
child working. Please try to
join us – Thursday or Friday.
I hope to hear from
you soon.
Sincerely,
Miss Gillon

FROM THE OFFICE OF THE PRINCIPAL

RE: *Curtis student/Shannon*

TO: *Miss Gillin*   DATE: *Oct. 22/88*

WITH REFERENCE TO: Issue of spelling / follow-up /
     complaint from parent (mother)

DOCUMENTATION:
     a) letter to Miss Gillin Oct. 12/88 from Mrs. Curtis
     b) responded to Mrs. Curtis Oct. 14/88 from Miss Gillin
     c) phone call to principal Oct.20/88 from Mrs. Curtis
  * d) phone call from principal to Mrs. Curtis

FOLLOW-UP: (To be completed by classroom teacher and
     returned to principal)

  *   to be discussed with teacher A.S.A.P.

COPY TO TEACHER ✓   COPY TO OFFICE ✓

Mr. Armstrong

FROM THE OFFICE OF THE PRINCIPAL

RE: Spelling program/Miss Gillin

DATE: October 29, 1988

RECOMMENDATIONS/FOLLOW-UP:

1. Weekly speller lessons/list of words
2. Immediate testing of Dolsch list
    for every student
3. Shannon tested - Mrs. Shantz - immediate
4. Pretest/post-test strategies
5. Feedback weekly to Mrs. Curtis; cc office files
6. Star chart re weekly spelling possibility

COPY TO TEACHER ✓   COPY TO OFFICE ✓

Mr. Armstrong

FROM THE OFFICE OF THE PRINCIPAL

DATE OF MEMO *Nv. 13/88*

TO: *Mrs Gillin*

REGARDING: *Curtis/Shannon*

_____

_____

(SEE ME)   (URGENT)   (A.S.A.P.) *Today*
                                            Recess

COPY TO TEACHER ✓   COPY TO OFFICE ✓

Mr. Armstrong

---

yestrday wen my dad he
cam hom he had wnt to
my unkel's place and
his car ~~but~~ has watr
in the gas line. my
dad fickoed the car.
                Shannon

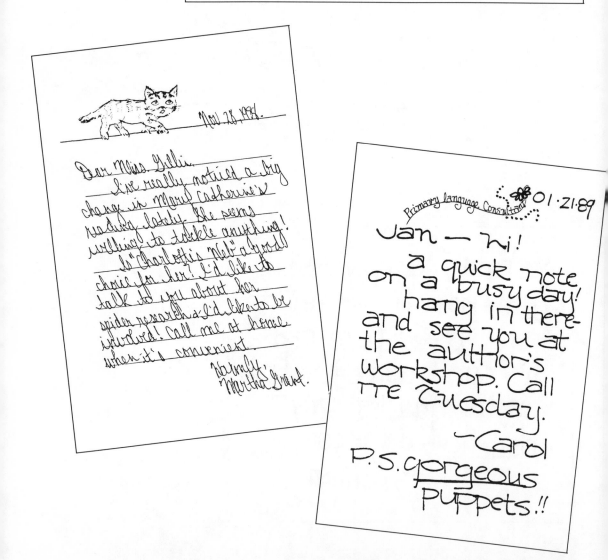

FILES FROM THE OFFICE OF THE PRINCIPAL

DATE OF MEMO: *Nov 19/88*

TO: *Miss Gilli*

REGARDING:

evaluation report, discussion and follow-up on the Curtis student

SEE ME   URGENT   A.S.A.P.

COPY TO TEACHER   COPY TO OFFICE

Mr. Armstrong

Nov 28, 1988.

Dear Miss. Gillis,
I've really noticed a big change in Mary Catherine's reading lately. She seems willing to tackle anything! Is "Charlotte's Web" a good choice for her? I'd like to talk to you about her spider research & I'd like to be involved! Call me at home when it's convenient.

Warmly,
Martha Grant.

Primary language Consultant 01·21·89

Jan — Hi!
a quick note on a busy day! hang in there — and see you at the author's workshop. Call me Tuesday.
— Carol
P.S. gorgeous puppets.!!

Primary Languge Consultant

hi everyone!
an invitation:
- Primary teachers swap and share night
- Feb 4/89 7 pm.
- Graham School
  〜 Carol
- Bring some recent writing samples.

page 2
One day they ꭓ ekskapd and the farmer he was redl madd. and they ran and ran to the nest farm. lets stay her sdid the chiken.

page 1 By Mary C.
Ons apon a time there waz a liddl piglit and he dident have eny frends. eksept for one chiken.

Dear Mr. Armstrong, Feb 29/89
    We had a really successful swap/share night with Carol last Tuesday and I think I have some new strategies to try with Shannon. I spoke with several other primary teachers and we have many common concerns about the spelling issue. When can we get together?

Miss Gillin.

FILES FROM THE OFFICE OF THE PRINCIPAL

MEMO: Re language/spelling issue

DATE OF MEMO: March 3, 1989

Dear Miss Gillin:

While I can appreciate your concerted efforts at maintaining a wholistic approach to spelling in your class structure per se, I cannot support your students' disregard for correct spelling in their creative writing and general language use in this school. It seems to me, that as educators, we need to carefully examine the model we display and realize that the underlying mistakes which we approve now, can indeed have crippling effects later on in life.

I am therefore requesting you to meet with me weekly to review your spelling instruction and implementation and I am enclosing a short term expectation to the end of March inclusive, so that lesson planning may be facilitated immediately.

Sincerely,

Mr. Armstrong

Mr. L. Armstrong
Principal

~~Last night~~
~~My Dad shot~~

Last night my dad
he shoed me ~~were where~~
the Oil is in the car and
Its got a long pece of medl
in it so you can tell when
it neds oil in the car.
Shannon.

gess what Mrs. Gillon!
I got a new jaket at
the kmart stor last nigt
and it has 99 like gretsky
on it. Its blue.
Shannon.
P.S. rit back soon.

DATE OF MEMO: April 5, 1989

Dear Miss Gillin:

I see very little progress in Shannon's spelling strategies, and as I reviewed your file, I see where the initial concern was raised by Mrs. Curtis was several months ago.

At our most recent meeting, you seemed to think that Shannon's visits to the resource teacher were only compounding his insecurities, and yet I can see no marked improvement by detaining him in the regular classroom.

In discussing his test results with Mrs. Shantz, the resource teacher, it is clear that he lacks most work attack skills, and appears to have no logical method for standard spelling development. This concern is of great tribulation to his mother, who has asked me on several occasions to address the issue with you.

This circumstance has reached a point where I feel it necessary to seek consultation and advisory assistance from the curriculum superintendent. I have contacted Mr. Richardson regarding the matter and have taken the liberty of securing an appointment with him on your behalf. He wishes to meet with you on Thursday April 18 at 4 p.m. I will arrange for Mr. Wilson to dismiss your students for you on that day.

Sincerely,

Mr. L. Armstrong
Principal

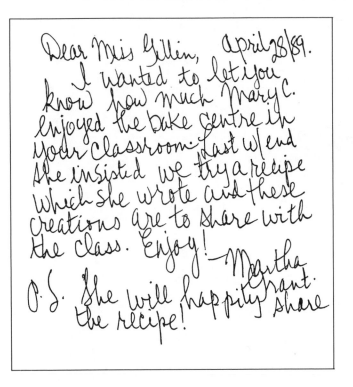

Dear Miss Gillin,   April 28/89.
I wanted to let you know how much Mary C. enjoyed the bake centre in your classroom. Last w/end she insisted we try a recipe which she wrote and these creations are to share with the class. Enjoy! — Martha Grant.

P.S. She will happily share the recipe!

May 4, 1989

Dear Mr. Armstrong,

Thank you for making the appointment for me to discuss the language and spelling concern with Mr. Richardson. With his approval, I invited Carol Shaw, our primary language arts consultant to join us at the meeting, and she provided some interesting insights into the improvements in Shannon's spelling strategies. At Mr.Richardson's request, I brought along several examples of Shannon's writing from September to December, as well as some of his more recent work. Our examination of his writing led us to some really exciting insights that I would like to share with you.

In September, Shannon rarely attempted to write anything at all. Despite continual invitations to respond via our letter center or message board, he seemed hesitant to join in. He was very conscious of a message reinforced at home: "I can't spell, so I can't write."

In November, he told the class about his father's service station and repair business, and one of the children asked him to draw a part of the car workings. This seemed to be a turning point for Shannon. We all encouraged him to share his knowledge about something he was interested in, and consequently, his first piece of writing evolved.

At our meeting on April 18, Mr. Richardson, Carol and I discussed at length the importance of allowing Shannon the freedom to explore spelling. If he had detected any hint of concern about the way he spelled the word <u>fixed</u> (fickesed), for example, he probably would not have tried to write the word at all. We concluded that it is necessary to reinforce the idea that spelling is not a crucial issue in initial writing. Of primary importance for me and for my students is that they write, and that they do not hesitate to take risks when trying to spell unfamiliar words.

Shannon is certainly displaying characteristics of an avid writer. He knows that spelling is important if the work is to be shared with someone who may not understand his spelling strategies. He is becoming an enthusiastic editor and we could see a concern for idea clarity in his writing.

My students and I would welcome you into our classroom at any time, Mr. Armstrong. We would like you to see us experimenting with writing, and we have many stories we'd love to share with you. I think you will agree that our writing is certainly serving a very worthwhile purpose. We are becoming better, clearer writers every time we pick up a pencil.

Sincerely,

Jan Gillin

Jan Gillin

June 4/89
4 pm

The room is quiet and I've been thinking about this whole business... Funny but today Shannon asked me how to spell Chevrolet — "I saw it on the back of my Dad's truck" he said, excitedly. I scribbled it down for him.

Hey! He's a member of the club whether he's in here with me or not — the important thing now is to keep letting him know what a great writer he is.

And principal? I know I'd handle that differently next time — not wait for him to invite himself — he won't. I need to invite him. No secrets in here — I want him to see us in action.

So what have you learned Gillin? ...that the greatest challenge is to help others understand why I do what I do. and I might not reach everyone — does Mrs. C understand a bit? I'll invite her in too someday soon — I wonder if she could've helped Shannon with the spelling of Chevrolet...

Jan.

PART SIX

changing

Trying to become a learner-directed and learning teacher is not easy. The transformation doesn't occur overnight or as a result of having attended an inservice workshop or two. No, changing our beliefs and practices is a messy, slow process, and there are relatively few supports for people as they try out new ideas. There aren't, for example, many opportunities for seeing how these ideas are actually being implemented. There are also limited opportunities for teachers to meet regularly and discuss what they're learning from their students. The prevailing inservice model is a transmission one: "tell 'em" and they'll understand. But the kind of change we've been describing here in *Finding Our Own Way* is far too complex for such an inservice strategy to have any impact at all.

Michael Coughlan describes how his experience as a graduate student helped him become aware of and change his set of working assumptions. Using a battle metaphor he explains how his defenses were finally breached.

121

Beverly Boone uses a fictitious correspondence with a friend to examine her personal growth as a result of her year of graduate study. She describes how learning in a collaborative context has helped her see her teaching role differently.

Sumitra Unia reflects on the problem of changing beliefs. A recent writing workshop she conducted makes her reconsider the complexities of helping teachers examine their assumptions and practices. She explores her own learning journey with teaching science and what she has learned about change from that experience.

19

A Belief System Under Siege
Michael Coughlan

A year ago, my classroom was my domain. I stood confident before my grade-seven social studies students, in firm (though sometimes not unquestioned) control. Things proceeded according to my careful plan.

With eight years of experience in the same school in the same subject areas, I knew how I wanted the class to function. I knew how I wanted to proceed with the teaching. Just as important, the students knew these things too. Oh, fate and the principal's office sometimes conspired to foil my well-laid plans, but I had learned to live with that. By and large, whenever I attempted teaching activities in class or out, I could fall back on tried-and-true procedures that I knew from experience would permit the fairly smooth flow of instruction.

I'm not suggesting I never had troubles. All teachers do, and I am no exception. But over time, problems arose less and less frequently. I developed a personal priority list of skills, topics, and concepts, and a corresponding repertoire of lessons to be covered each year. This personal guidebook of mine grew from ideas gleaned from inservices, other teachers, and official guides and texts, but mostly, I acted on some gut feeling about what and how things should be taught. This personal guidebook was the result of testing done in the field, under fire. It had cost a lot in sweat and tears to develop. It's not easy to give up a thing like that.

And yet I did. Not completely. I found new ideas to take the place of the old. That turned out to be very important in the end. The realization that I wasn't leaving myself with a void somewhat soothed my fear of "starting over."

Over the course of this past year, most of my personal guidebook has been challenged. Like some great fortress under seige, my preconceived notions about learning were systematically overthrown, one by one. The assault was not a frontal one; that would have resulted ultimately in increased resistance on my part. No, my beliefs were breached, and their eventual downfall came when the foundations were undermined. For some ideas, I fought tooth and nail, while others fell with barely a whimper.

No single one of these beliefs stands out as my major bastion of resistance. I can see the beliefs were connected, lending support to each other; my own unconscious Maginot Line. And like that other defense network, reassuringly safe as long as the assumptions were allowed to stand.

The first shock was that I really had some underlying theory lurking in my head, affecting the way I functioned in my classroom. Yes, I possessed a theory of learning—every teacher does. I had come to university to acquire one and had found my own homegrown version fully developed within me, adopted unconsciously, unwittingly, over the years in the classroom. Not me, you say, I don't pay any attention to that theoretical nonsense. Well, I discovered I had indeed functioned with a very definite theory of learning, although I could not put much of it into words before. But actions speak louder than words, especially when dealing with students.

What shook these assumptions I held? What made the shift of view possible? Well, in part, the manner in which I was instructed in my graduate classes. No one told me the right answers. In fact, everybody kept saying there weren't any, and they were supposed to be the experts. Instead, in assigned readings I was confronted with various divergent opinions about reading and writing. I was not expected to read for the right answers, but to form my own opinion on the particular issue addressed by the selections. The readings often became a subtle prod, stimulating my own thinking. Daily writing about these articles became another tool for consolidating my own understanding of the issues. No one corrected me, though my ideas were often questioned. In struggling to stem this determined assault, I was forced to confront what I honestly felt about issues.

I found my position untenable as I tried to mend the breach. Each time I struggled to counter various authors' opinions, I recognized strong demonstrations of the opposing arguments reflected in my past and present learning experiences. How had they known I hadn't followed the advice of my writing teachers for years? I had never written from detailed outlines. In fact if outlines were required, I often had completed them after the piece was written. I had often written a history term paper, then taken it apart and reshuffled the pieces to make it sound better. And I had often found that it didn't say what I had originally intended. Looking within to see the learning process at work, I recognized in myself the embodiment of a transactional theory of reading and writing. I had to decide: surrender the point or cling stubbornly to my crumbling battlements, despite the lack of cover. In the end, I had to be honest with myself.

The fiercest struggle raged over the manner in which language develops. I had always assumed reading and writing were too complex to be learned all at once. Only after each skill was mastered could it become incorporated into the students' writing and reading. This rarely happened in practice, of course, but I never once doubted my emphasis on teaching skills in isolation. I carefully pointed out students' errors so they would learn not to repeat them. How else would they learn to use the grammar, punctuation, and spelling needed to communicate clearly? There was simply too much to leave to chance.

I refused to believe that writing skills could be learned incidentally until I began to look at how I had learned historical methodology. Most of the conventions of historical research were never explicitly taught to me, as far as I can remember, by anyone. Yet I picked up enough historical research techniques along the way to do well in university. Not once can I recall a teacher explaining the way a history paper should read, or how to use primary evidence to support suppositions and generalizations. The point is, though, I did learn how to handle the genre of academic research papers, at least well enough to satisfy my instructors. I had never really considered where that knowledge came from, except to say from "experience."

The answer suggested by several writers, especially Frank Smith (1982), was that the exposure to the genre itself can show learners how a research paper should read. I now realized I had incidentally learned a lot about historiography, about testing and supporting hypotheses, and about writing, through the reading I'd done even though my intention had been to learn some history. This was a crucial connection for me. Seeing incidental learning at work within myself allowed me to back away from class instruction in grammar, punctuation, and spelling since I've understood that in the process of writing and reading for their own research and creative purposes, students will acquire knowledge of the conventions of language when it is important and necessary for them to do so.

I don't believe in leaving everything to chance, though. While helping students write stories and research papers, I can see many opportunities for teaching skills that are useful for writing. This means spending more class time writing and adjusting my teaching to reflect the needs and purposes of my students.

This introduces another factor that slowed my adoption of a new theory of learning. I was coming to accept the assertions of an interpretive perspective, but I was unable to see how I could implement my changing views in the classroom. Although I could accept the changes on a rational, theoretical level, I was uncomfortable abandoning my old personal guidebook. I was comfortable with my old ways, and what was more, I knew that, by and large, they were successful. That is, they helped me maintain control of the students and produced some evidence of learning. What helped me overthrow this last pocket of resistance was the realization that all those years of experience weren't a waste. They provided a foundation upon which to build a whole new structure. I didn't have to throw away all the old bricks in my walls; I only had to rearrange the material to reflect what I now believe about learning.

Reference

Smith, Frank. 1982. *Writing and the Writer.* New York: Holt, Rinehart and Winston.

Fear, Risk, and Change: Reflections on a Year as Learner

Beverly R. Boone

April 27

Dear Gloria,

Thank you for your letter. Believe it or not, it helped me realize just how important my year of study has been.

You wondered why I would torture myself by returning to graduate school. After all, I had a job. I already had an education degree and was fulfilling quite capably the many duties required by the teaching positions I've held during the past fourteen years. Why did I need a year off to study? The truth is, I was unhappy with how I was teaching. I didn't feel comfortable with what I was doing and thought it was time to learn more.

I must confess I enrolled in the reading program here expecting to be told how to teach reading and writing. That's what I experienced as an undergraduate and at those workshops, inservices, and conferences. I certainly didn't expect to have any input into how and what I learned. But after the first week of classes, I quickly realized that I, indeed, was expected to take control and that the courses were going to be very different from any I had taken previously.

I've listened to very few lectures. Instead, I have been reading, writing, and talking far more than I bargained for. This unnerved me at first, but I quickly became comfortable with the work. It didn't matter whether I remembered everything I read. I wasn't expected to regurgitate right answers. The collaboration among all of us in class was more important.

I remember talking to a couple of the other teachers at registration and hearing them mention something called "whole language." I didn't have a clue what they were talking about at the time, although I pretended I did. I was concerned about that, afraid I was behind before I began. I recognize now, though, that I didn't have to worry about anyone having a head start. We weren't competing with one another. Indeed, our varying backgrounds and experiences proved an asset; we had a lot to share.

An important aspect of the program this year has been the opportunity I've been given to reflect on many incidents that occurred in my classroom over the years. Looking back, I immediately think of two students: Paul and Angela. Paul was an enigma for me. He could do any social studies, science, or math activity, but he just couldn't do the comprehension exercises. For two years, he watched as classmates moved to the next grade without him. He tried so hard but all of the phonics and comprehension drills I thought would cure him did more harm than good. Yes, I believed then that the only way he was going to learn to read was if I taught him skills. You know—to get him to learn lists of spelling words and to complete pages from workbooks.

Then there was Angela. She never quite figured out how to play the game of giving the answer I wanted. I thought it was so cute when her mother told me on parent night that Angela thought I kept "the big book with all the right answers" somewhere on my desk. I understand now what she was really telling me.

I also understand that most of my students were doing things not because of any intrinsic interest but because I set the assignments and graded them. Most of them had no personal investment in what we were doing. How many times could I, and should I, have questioned why they were passing in work with the very same mistakes I'd carefully corrected numerous times before? I didn't bother to ask, because I assumed it was their fault they weren't learning; it certainly wasn't mine. And that matter of mistakes. I guess I've learned from my own experiences as a student that mistakes are a natural part of learning. Although it may be too late for me to help Paul and Angela, I'm certain there will be others I can help with these new insights.

I've taken lots of risks this year. My first and most important one was deciding to return to study. I realize now that a large part of my anxiety about becoming a student came from being afraid to admit I didn't know what I was doing a good deal of the time and believing someone else could tell me the answers.

You see, Gloria, while I've had a difficult year, I've learned a great deal. I've reexamined what I thought teaching was all about; I've come to see being a teacher in new ways. I'm excited about teaching next year, although I still have qualms: If I change how I teach, will the students learn what they're supposed to? Will they measure up academically to the other classes? Will I ever get the content covered? Will I fit in with the others on the staff?

Good thing I love a challenge. I don't see the learning experience I've had this year ending in June when I finish the program. Instead, I face a new beginning.

Sincerely,

Bev

Time for Change
Sumitra Unia

"My students keep making the same mistakes even after we correct them in a writing conference. I also find talking to every student takes too long," complained Louise, a grade-two teacher. She was attending, with other elementary teachers, the second of three inservice days on reading and writing planned for the year by the school district. During the previous inservice in September, she and the others had engaged in some writing themselves. They'd listed topics they wanted to write about, talked about them within their groups, written, and discussed how talking had helped them write. The focus of that session had been on clarifying content to help the teachers discover the importance of talk in developing writing fluency. Nevertheless, Louise was still concerned about conventions. Like many of the other teachers, she was devoting a good deal of her time to correcting children's mistakes during her conferences. She was having trouble differentiating between helping the children develop content and editing.

As the teachers talked about the sorts of things they had learned from what they had been trying with their students, the discrepancy between the instructional changes we were attempting to implement in the district and what was actually happening in classrooms was evident. I had a strong sense of futility as the hour drew to a close. We were trying to initiate a change in teachers' understanding about writing. But there was far too little time to bring about such a complex change. Three inservice days, spread across nine months, was inadequate for helping teachers reflect on their instruction. We barely had time to describe the theoretical beliefs behind writing conferences, let alone offer demonstrations of various kinds of conferences, discuss their efforts to implement writing conferences, or actually assist them in their classrooms. We were attempting a substantial change without providing the time and intensive support required.

129

When the inservice session was over, I thought about my own professional development. My understanding of learning as a dynamic process began when I heard about open classrooms and discovery learning in the early seventies. Unfortunately, no one showed me how to set a discovery-learning context in motion. Nor did I seek out teachers who were successfully implementing such change, lest my inadequacies become public and my own image of competence be tarnished. I was operating under the traditional illusion of the teacher as an expert, and I continued my struggle in isolation.

Science was the first area of the curriculum I ventured to change. I scrounged around for materials and set up small-group hands-on activities to help my students learn instead of watching the weekly educational program on television. The noise level of my students worried me, since I was afraid it reflected poor discipline. However, convinced of the value of experiential learning, I persisted. I also began using concrete materials in math at about the same time.

The one-day inservices in science and math in those days were helpful because I was already on the alert for ways to change how I taught. Although I was self-directed, I was unaware of the possibility or importance of follow-up and support for effective implementation. It was hard to go beyond the standard textbooks, to use a variety of print and nonprint materials. I had so little time to read *Learning*, my first professional journal, let alone try the ideas I found in it.

I only began to appreciate the importance of learning through sharing after a colleague and I became interested in outdoor education to extend our science teaching. At first, we took our grade-four and -five students for one-day excursions. Later, we made yearly overnight camping trips. Our outdoor education collaboration led to other cooperative endeavors. We began talking about language arts and math instruction. As Reta and I worked more and more closely at increasing opportunities for active learning, our students became more enthusiastic and involved. However, I still had a few students who continued having difficulty with the reading program. To help them, I began looking for alternatives.

Reta suggested trying individualized reading. My principal lent me a book to read. With her encouragement, I obtained some funding from the province to buy books. She also helped me find and order other materials. At an open-house night, parents were invited to see the new materials their children would be using for reading. So with the support of my friend, the principal, and the community, I started to implement an individualized reading program.

Individualized reading seemed to offer the students more scope. My students wrote daily reports about what they were reading, and I talked with them regularly, focusing mainly on meaning. I also spent some time instructing small groups in specific skills. However, I did find it extremely difficult to meet with all of the children individually each week. In addition, because the students were writing reports about what they were reading, I also discussed their writing with them, although I was still attending primarily to correcting what they wrote.

I started to see language arts in terms of process rather than product, largely as a result of the graduate courses I began taking. Belonging to a teachers' voluntary study group helped me sustain and further develop changes in language arts instruction. I learned from what my friends were changing in their classrooms and how they were going about it. I began to appreciate the importance of collaborating with colleagues. We shared our successes, concerns, and problems in our monthly meetings and returned to the classroom invigorated.

However, my understanding of effective educational change began only after an elementary science expert chose my school to demonstrate the advantages of long-term, school-based inservice. In collaboration with my principal and the science consultant for the city, she undertook to provide inservice in science over a three-year period. During that time, we learned about process teaching in science, using hands-on materials. We learned about content from small-group experiences that encouraged observing, inferring, and classifying—ways of recording and evaluating progress. We met with our leaders in between the workshops to share ideas or to iron out problems. The principal scheduled the timetable so teachers at each grade level could get together weekly. We made up kits of materials necessary to teach different units at each grade level. The effort was coordinated and supported throughout the school over an extended period of time. This experience was unique. The skills and strategies we were to learn were clearly defined and demonstrated in the hands-on activities we participated in. The time and support we were given allowed us to experience, understand, and implement this change and earned our strong commitment to hands-on science instruction.

The science experience reinforced my ideas about child-centered learning in language arts. Being a teacher-learner during the science inservices made teaching that subject more meaningful and easier. I could now see the importance of being a writer myself in order to teach my students how to write. With the support of my study group, I began to write along with my students. Research articles stressing the importance of teachers being writers also made my active participation imperative. I began to see language as a medium for learning; language development a consequence of using language to learn. With renewed enthusiasm, I encouraged children to write across the curriculum.

My instructional practice has been slowly evolving for a number of years now. Nevertheless, when I reflect critically, as I have had the occasion to do frequently this past year, I still observe inconsistencies between what I believe and what I actually do in the classroom. I am beginning to understand the importance of my role as a teacher-learner-researcher.

Change has to be meaningful before people can feel committed to bringing it about. Even when we agree on the need for change, we must establish clearly what it will involve. To make the writing inservices with the district teachers more meaningful, we have to consider the teachers' experiences and needs. We need to discover the obstacles the teachers perceive in translating this change into practice and to help them develop strategies for overcoming them. Only by planning a long-term implementation, closely monitoring and supporting its growth, can we bring about significant improvement in our current writing instruction.

PART SEVEN

taking a risk

There comes a point when the teachers in the "Writing and Computers" class take a deep breath and jump in. They realize they can no longer continue teaching as they have been. The time has come to "just have a go." That is a difficult moment. It means giving up security. It involves taking a risk. What's scary about making ourselves vulnerable is that it might not work—something unexpected might occur, and then what do we do? There is a built-in safety net, though. Being open to learning from our students provides the feedback that allows us to sustain the learning enterprise.

Janice Clarke describes several innovations she decided to try with students in her French classes. By adapting some curricular ideas she's read about and heard discussed in connection with English language arts instruction, she's begun a collaborative journey with her students.

Linda Cook describes a few of the major changes she intends implementing in her classroom. She takes a close look at a number of tried-and-true practices and explains why she has decided to abandon them.

22

I Don't Know Enough French!

Janice L. Clarke

There is a hum of low-key conversation, accompanied by the scratching of twenty-five pencils at work as these grade-five students write mystery descriptions of a fellow classmate. Occasionally, someone asks a question. Another student answers. What makes this situation so special is that these are Anglophone students in my French classroom. I have told them they will have the opportunity to read their descriptions to the class. We, in turn, will try to guess the identity of the mystery person.

"Madame, can we write more than one description?" asks one student.

"Yes," I answer. The children cheer and work even more industriously.

"Madame, do we get to present all of our descriptions?"

"Yes," I again reply. They continue writing eagerly.

The grade-six students enter the classroom, their excitement evident as they view the brown manila envelope in my hand. They take their seats impatiently. One of them can keep quiet no longer.

"Are those our pen-pal letters, Madame?"

"Yes."

The students chatter excitedly as I distribute the letters, written in French.

"Listen to what my pen pal wrote. . . ."

"Hey, mine likes the same sports as I do!"

"Can we write them back *now*, Madame?"

They arrange themselves in small support groups of four or five, where problems encountered as they write their replies will first be addressed. Working quickly and quietly, they share ideas and answers. I circulate around the classroom, comment on their efforts, and answer queries that the group cannot solve. When the thirty-minute class has ended, all but two of the twenty-four have their replies ready to be mailed. As the students leave the room, their main concern is when they will be getting the answering letters back.

Twenty-eight grade-four students are seated quietly, listening to their two classmates at the front of the room. David is playing the role of a famous talk-show host, about to introduce us to his celebrity guest, played by Jason. The dialogue is in French.

David: *Bonjour, Alf. Ça va aujourd'hui?*
(Hello, Alf. How are you today?)
Jason: *Très bien, merci.*
(Great, thanks.)
David: *D'òu viens-tu, Alf?*
(Where are you from, Alf?"
Jason: *Je viens de la planete Melmac.*
(I come from the planet Melmac.)
David: *Est-ce que tu aimes les chats, Alf?*
(Do you like cats, Alf?)
Jason: *Bien sûr! J'aime beaucoup les chats! Je mange les chats tout le temps!*
(Of course! I love cats! I eat cats all the time!)

The interview continues; the audience enjoys the show. Now, it's another pair's turn. I wonder what roles they have chosen to play today. Peewee Herman? Samantha Fox? The class becomes impatient between conversations. They are just as anxious to hear what their classmates have prepared as they are to present their own work.

These situations have one common thread—they occurred in my French classroom this year. I was the one who set the guidelines, but the students had to decide how they wanted to proceed within those parameters. This is the first time I've tried to give my students any amount of control over their own learning, and it's a bit scary, I have to admit. Unlike using workbook pages and drill exercises, there is an element of the unknown involved in giving students control. Surprises become the norm, not the exception.

My recent reading had made me feel uncomfortable with the way I was teaching. I have come to believe that exchanges of information among students are necessary for learning. This, however, created a problem for me, since I was supposed to be creating as "pure" a French environment in my classroom as I possibly could. Yet in order to encourage conversation among students, I had to allow the use of English. Their vocabulary skills were just not adequate to maintain a totally French classroom discussion. When the students took more control, I saw them learning from each other, not only by supplying vocabulary and explanations, but also by sharing ideas and problems. They could then start to use their French to communicate with one another.

My students' increased enthusiasm has been another noticeable result of having given them more responsibility for their own learning. They are now eager to try new things; they've lost most of the inhibitions that were in evidence last September. Like toddlers who have begun to do things for themselves, my students are gaining more independence with every new adventure tackled in the classroom. They have begun to draw on resources besides me to aid them. They search out dictionaries, other books, and each other when they need help. They are no longer restricted to one strategy— seeking the teacher when they have a question to be answered.

Not all of my problems are being encountered in the classroom, either. The lack of research material on teaching a second language through a holistic approach has left me exploring virtually uncharted waters. I have had to adopt the double role of teacher and researcher as I have gradually felt my way through this year. And even though my department is generally supportive, I have not tried to explain to them all the changes I'm currently experiencing in my classroom. To teach as I now do has required a change in how I view the process of learning. This is too difficult to try to explain to someone who has not undergone the same metamorphosis. Instead, I'm researching and documenting as I teach, so I can answer challenges should they arise at a later date.

I don't have all the bugs worked out yet and seriously doubt that I ever will. But my classes and I have had a lot of fun learning together this year. I have a new respect for my students as learners. Now, I rarely hear the comment, "I don't know enough French!"

23

A Letter to the Principal
Linda Cook

September 6, 1988

Dear Mr. Hunter,

Thank you for welcoming me back to school after my year's sabbatical. The opening staff meeting made me feel as if I had never been away. That was a cute remark about my being "born again at the Mount," and did you really mean it when you said I might "lead the flock" with a PTWL (Praise The Whole Language) hotline?

Actually, I was thinking how rested you looked since your summer vacation: tanned and full of the usual zest after a couple of months off from the "salt mine." I don't want to rock the boat and activate the old stomach problems, but I have been wondering if I might modify the requests on the requisition form you want returned by the end of the month. I have always found the sixty dollars a tremendous boon toward the purchase of supplies, but I am thinking, in terms of my changed outlook, it could be better spent in other ways.

The following are a few changes I would like to make to my usual requests:

1. Stickers. You must remember my master plan: my system of sticker motivation that set up a sort of Wheel-of-Fortune every month. Well, I've given it considerable thought, and I no longer think it useful. I know it was very popular; it was a prototype for other teachers to adopt, but it was getting out of hand, logistically as well as financially. Each month, I had to provide a new supply of assorted stickers—plain ones worth one point, smelly ones worth two points. Ballots had to be made and issued on the total month's points for each student—every five points equaled a ballot that would give a student a chance on the Big Draw. The bookkeeping alone was unwieldy. I dreaded those afternoons where students buddied up to

139

check whether fake stickers had been counted or sneaked into total scores. The classroom would be in chaos with the bickering that erupted over the inevitable sticker controversy. Then, that evening, I would have to drag myself through the stores in search of some item that would excite the kids. You talk about headaches, Mr. Hunter!

Each month's prize would have to be bigger and better than the last. It got so the students would not work unless there was some payment. Parents were beginning to complain that they were finding it hard to get their kids to do homework unless they were promised a prize. One of the students even asked, "What's a note to Grandma worth?"

Having thought about the contradictions this sticker lotto creates, I've decided it would be much better buying materials students need for editing their stories, that is, marking pens, paper, scissors, tape, glue, rulers—all those things we need in large supply for our editing corner. You see, I've learned the stickers were merely reinforcing the concept that learning was so terrible it had to be rewarded. I was teaching students to learn the wrong things.

2. I would like to replace the homework notebook. I know you thought it was a good idea, and parents commended me for my diligence in following up every assignment by checking it against their signatures. But really, what good does policing do the faithful, trustworthy students who keep being punished by having to repeat the practice nightly? It would be much better to let their positive attitudes rub off on the offenders, rather than the other way around. At least now, I won't have to be suspicious of Johnny copying his mother's signature, which is what I was predisposing him to do. Raising little forgers is certainly not my intention!

Now, what I would like instead concerns our computer, the Commodore 64, which is collecting too much dust in the office. The teachers have mentioned that it is rarely used, despite everyone's pitching in to buy it with the money we received for taking over the noon-hour duty. The trouble is, the trolley on which the computer sits has no wheels and is pretty heavy to lift. It takes four bigger kids, two on either side, to move it. The maintenance supervisor is adamant about our not pushing it down the hallway, since this makes black marks across the tiles. Four castors would not be unduly expensive and would give our Commodore mobility, not to mention the extra space you'd gain in your office. Since I've learned to use a computer, I realize anyone can learn, and the students will be whizzes in no time if they have the chance.

3. I would like to have the money I normally used for workbooks to accompany the basal reader reallotted to a classroom typewriter. I won't need the workbooks because I don't plan to use the basal reader, either. I'm embarking, instead, on a program using real books based on the interests of my students. I can understand your wondering if this sabbatical has shaken my logic. You see, I have decided not to go with the workbooks despite all the time they saved me having to find follow-up activities to the stories. They definitely were convenient, each page laid out with blanks to fill in, words to match, and questions to answer. The students were never idle.

They always went about their work, knowing exactly what to do, since they had done the same things the day before. The exercises were so predictable, the students didn't have to think. A gem to correct too.

However, if you think back to the spring of '87, when the workmen were outside your window, drilling a hole for the new flagpole, how did you feel? Be honest. Remember that continuous drilling? I can't let you forget your remark when you thundered out into the hall, bellowing that it was the same thing day after day and that there had to be an easier way. "A man can't think!" you exclaimed. Exactly the same for the students—only the pounding is on their heads and not on the pavement. I can't go on breaking up language into fragments, expecting my students to be drilled and filled. I wonder what would have happened to our children if we'd given them lessons and workbook skills on how to talk or walk? We really would have problems on our hands!

Just consider this instead. My classroom floor, with clusters of grade-four students collaborating over how they might work something out in their writing or running to the shelves to find how real authors express themselves or perhaps using a variety of strategies to make their writing purposeful and meaningful. And then, the typewriter on a table of its own for the young publisher. I can see those deft fingers feeling for the keys, which when learned will make the students more adept on the keyboard of the computer.

4. My last request won't cost anything. You see, for some time now, I've been longing for a cozier atmosphere in my classroom—one that evokes childhood memories of snuggling up on the Chesterfield with a great book. No, I'm not asking for an armchair, but I am angling for the construction of a nook, perhaps a "treehouse," that some of the parents might want to build in either corner at the back of the classroom. Feeling they would interfere with my teaching, I have always shied away from asking for parents' help, but I realize I can't do without them and that I need their expertise. Could you imagine my building a treehouse, Mr. Hunter? I would like to have carpet ends and a few throw cushions around. Presto! A place where dreams might germinate. If the truth be known, I've always wanted my own treehouse.

I am looking forward to the year ahead. My year of study has revitalized me and opened my eyes to how much fun learning can be. I hope I can share this with the kids. If you have any questions, you'll know where to find me.

Until the next staff meeting,

Sincerely,

Linda

PART EIGHT

journeying

I'm uncomfortable when I hear people announce "I'm *doing* whole language." Some kind of retort is wanted, but I realize the absence of reflection that's evident in that statement is rarely the fault of the teacher. The misconception that whole language is just another instructional approach is widespread. I frequently encounter fellow teacher-educators who are writing and doing presentations on "*the* whole language *approach*." So I ought not to be surprised, I guess, when I hear teachers say they're *doing* whole language. To counteract this distortion of what is fundamentally a philosophical perspective, I expend a great deal of energy engaging people in a reflective process. From beginning to end in the "Writing and Computers" class, people are asked to examine their beliefs about learning and about teaching. That investigation is often unnerving, but once they begin questioning their assumptions, a door opens and the teachers can see many instructional possibilities. They realize that by adopting an interpretive, learner-directed stance,

143

we are embarking on a never-ending journey. There can be no arriving because the road goes ever on.

Fred Williams didn't intend "The Key" as a piece for *Finding Our Own Way*, but when I read it I was struck by his synthesis of his experience in the "Writing and Computers" class and the form he chose for writing about it. One reader thought it unfortunate that the importance of group collaboration wasn't included in his description. That omission was caused largely by the circumstances under which the piece was written: Fred was writing to share with me his personal insights as a result of our journey together. In this retrospective, his focus is on himself and what he learned from his experiences in the course. In fact, without the supportive, collaborative context that was built through our collective discussion and sharing, Fred would never have written the piece at all.

To Fred, then, the last word.

The Key
Fred Williams

"You too, eh?" chuckled the innkeeper, an old man. "Can't say that I can do much for you. Been a mighty long line of folks through here lately. Never see many of them again."

The traveler stood by the counter, looking at the face of the old man.

"Can you give me some direction," said the traveler, "some advice? I need to find the Key."

The old man was quiet, considering if, or how, to respond to the plea. Then, in a measured tone, he began. "The challenge you've set for yourself is difficult but not impossible. The Key has been sought by many—not always with success. The journey is rough. Between here and there are deserts that'll evaporate your blood, mountains that'll wear you out, and creatures so jealous of their territory you'd swear it was their sacred mission to protect the Key. Even if you get through, there's no guarantee you'll find it. Like I said, haven't seen many back this way. Got lost I guess—or worse."

The traveler was slightly shaken. There was time to turn back, he thought. No one was forcing him to undertake this quest. Dammit, wasn't there an easier way?

The innkeeper looked through the window, down the long plain to the mountains. "You know," he said, not looking at the traveler, "beginning here means you pass through several dangerous zones."

The traveler had heard rumors.

"Zones 698 and 699 will wear you down," the innkeeper continued, "and 629 demands you deal with experiences you thought best forgotten. Those who have been there say it's rough."

The traveler wanted to leave; the innkeeper's tone was beginning to irritate him. This was not the way to begin a quest.

"If you have any suggestions at all ..." said the traveler, working toward the door.

"I have," the innkeeper offered. "Get yourself a good guide."

The traveler leaned against the fence and waited for someone to show. The heat made him irritable, and he didn't like these blind meetings. He had only the innkeeper's word that someone would meet him.

Just then, a figure emerged from the inn and stopped between him and the sun, feet planted, hands on hips.

"Hi, my name is Judith. I'm your guide."

Out of the heat, they talked. He noticed the guide's kite brooch, the leather tunic, and the survival kit with its contents neatly arranged. She was prepared. It gave him confidence.

He wanted to know more about the Key. She was a guide, she said, someone who leads, but the client should set the goal.

They struck a contract. She could be with him only one day a week, and then maybe two if the schedule worked out. She passed him a small communication device, a Voicevax, she called it. If he needed support when she was not around, he could contact her. No promises, just a commitment to help negotiate the pitfalls of the Zones.

He set off, alone, but with a set of directions: keep the mountains ahead and maintain a regular account of your experience.

He questioned the value of the directions, but for now, accepted them on faith. His determination to find the Key carried him, yet he remained cautious, walking only in the day and keeping the mountains in plain view.

One day, the traveler came early to an oasis, fresh and with much of the day remaining. A dilemma—should he stay here and relax or should he push on? He decided to continue, impatient to conclude the journey. However, darkness caught him in the middle of nowhere. He could not see the mountains. Yet a light ahead eased his anxiety. He half ran to the beacon, finding the entrance to some subterranean passage.

He entered. The door closed behind him. A faceless figure in monk's robes sat at a table. The traveler turned to leave. The door was locked. He was a prisoner.

"Approach," the monk said.

The traveler moved hesitantly to the table.

"Your logs, please."

Opening his sack, he placed his journals on the table. The monk began to read, writing notes in the margin with pencil. He worked quickly. Laying the pencil aside he asked, "What is the purpose of this log?"

The traveler did not respond. It had no purpose. It was an instruction to be followed. He was obeying his guide.

"Your journey cannot continue till you come to some understanding of this enterprise."

The monk disappeared, leaving the traveler to sort out the meaning of the encounter.

The traveler went to the door, knowing that it would not open. He sat in the chair, the monk's words twisting in his head. Looking at his logs, he saw questions, all questions, nothing else.

Each day he tried the door. Each day he searched his journals: descriptions of the weather, the hardships, the dangers.... Nothing in his writing presented itself as a solution. In his despair, he wrote of his captivity, "What is it I believe? Why am I here?"

The door swung open. Air and brilliant light flooded the chamber. The traveler seized his logs and ran out into the day. That night, in his log, he did not describe the darkness; he questioned what he could learn from it.

The following Tuesday, Judith appeared. He told her of his adventure. She seemed unalarmed. Together, they planned the next leg of the journey. She read his logs and wrote reactions and questions in the margins. When she left camp, he read the notes. Some of her questions angered him. Why should he think of an alternate way to make a fire? His method was perfectly reliable. What did it matter how he did things on a previous journey? This is the one that matters. Why should he consider changing?

He was in the mountains now, the thirst and exhaustion of the plain behind, replaced by icy paths, cold, deathly rocks, and deep gulches. He cursed these God-forsaken zones, wanting often to turn back. Still, he believed in the existence of the Key. His logs now dealt with the personal issues of his survival.

As he walked through the dead grass of a long meadow and enjoyed the sure footing and crisp, autumn weather, his world gave way from under him. He plunged into a pit, his hands grasping to break his fall. A ledge stopped his plummet. He was on his back, the pit opening ten feet above. He eased to a sitting position. Nothing broken, he thought. Just then, he sensed a movement—the walls of the pit were moving. His eyes slowly focused on knots of slithering, stretching, coiling snakes. In the dim light, he was able to see blue, green, red, and brown reptiles—leather belts, he thought—moving on the ledges above him, each ledge a different color. He was prisoner again.

He could climb to the lip of the pit but the snakes might be poisonous. Movement might be fatal. His ledge was the furthest into the hole. All the snakes were above him, close to the late autumn sun. Would they move down into the depths as night approached?

Slowly and silently, he removed his knapsack. He found the Voicevax and sent out a distress call. Judith responded immediately. Be a while before she could get there. Stay put, she said. Watch the snakes and get an idea of their habits. Record your observations and then make a decision.

The snakes stayed high in the pit. At first light he took out his notebook and thought about what he should look for. Did they look like the poisonous snakes with which he was familiar? Were they taking food? How far did they move away from their ledge? Which seemed the biggest? Fastest?

The watching and waiting began. For three days, he read the situation and made notes as the snakes twisted above him. The reds blocked the easiest way to the surface, but they were poisonous. A mouse had fallen to their ledge and one touch of the fangs killed it instantly. A brown struck a shrew but the star-nosed creature struggled all the way to the snake's stomach. The browns were sluggish, rarely moving from their ledge. The greens were large and explored the pit, coming uncomfortably close to the interloper. The blues, though lethal and far-ranging, didn't move till the sun was directly over the pit. His observations determined his course: the most difficult, but safest route was through the browns.

On the fourth day, early morning, he edged his way up the wall of the pit and came eye-to-eye with the browns. He stopped whenever a red or blue stirred. It took him painful hours. His body was sore from the tension. Finally, he kicked his feet over the rim and lay on his back. Reaching behind, his hand covered a shiny, silver brooch.

In the following weeks, the traveler penetrated the mountains without incident. The brooch didn't become an issue; he slipped it into Judith's kit on one of her stops. She must have reasons for letting him pass those terrible hours in the pit. There was much he didn't understand, but a pact had been established.

The exercise hardened his body, and he had deeper insights into his experience. But his journal was riddled with doubts. When would the questions stop coming? When would he break free from this forbidding land and find the Key?

He came to a canyon through which roared a spitting, angry river. It seemed impassable. He walked upstream, looking for a way across. The noise of the spate was deafening. After days of searching, he found a rope bridge that spanned the torrent hundreds of feet below.

A small hut with an iron entry guarded the bridge. The tinny, level voice of a droid halted the traveler: "State your business."

The traveler had never before spoken to a mechanical intelligence. Self-consciously he said, "I want to cross the river. I am in search of the Key."

"No one crosses without passing a test. Please take this sheet and return it to me when you're done. If you respond correctly, we will consider your request."

The traveler sat on a rock and read the paper. It had two tasks: the first, a freewrite, and the second, an account, for publication and for an audience of fellow travelers, of what was learned on the journey. It seemed straightforward enough. Within an hour, he had delivered the first task to the droid.

"Approved," said the droid, and the traveler rushed into the second task, confident it would go as well. However, when he delivered it to the droid, the response set him back.

"You are telling, not showing," said the droid. "How about trying again?"

Ah, well, a few changes here and there shouldn't take him long. Two hours later, he passed the droid a second draft.

"Could use some incidents," said the droid, in that flat, irritating voice.

What in the hell was going on? This exercise was beginning to annoy him. The traveler took the piece and revised it, fleshing it out with experiences. Surely that would do. His gait was less confident as he approached the hut this time.

"Too busy now. Needs more focus," said the droid.

Like hell, thought the traveler. This is it. No more. This computer doesn't know what it wants. He sat on the rim of the canyon, sulking, looking at the woods on the other side. He began to hate the writing and the droid-editor, but he had to get moving. He reworked the piece, shifting material, deleting, and trying to deal with a single issue.

"You're close," said the robot. "Try playing with the ending now."

The traveler did a wild dance of jubilation. He sat on his rock to consider the ending and only then admitted the influence of the editor on his work.

This piece is not meant to end, he thought. How could he show that? Punctuation? That was one way. Borrowing a technique he had seen somewhere else, he inserted a comma and rushed to the tollbridge to deliver the copy.

The droid took a long time reading it.

"Pass," said the droid, and the iron gate lifted to allow him entry.

Where were the boundaries? How could the traveler tell one zone from another? The territory looked the same. Nowhere did he see a line, a signpost, a distance marker, a map. On other journeys these distinctions had always been laid out for him.

Judith visited regularly, listening and responding to his concerns, returning his logs and leaving hers. He was able to see how she plotted her course. It was helpful. One day he asked her, "How do I know these things for myself?"

"Look within," she said. "Only you can truly answer these questions; I can't answer them for you. I have an idea of your position and how far you've come, but I suspect you do too. Look to the questions, not the answers."

She left camp, leaving him with some direction. Still the questions: What have you learned on this journey? What insights have you had? He ignored them at first, but as the journey lengthened, those simple queries provided focus.

There is no earthly way through these mountains, he thought. For days he had followed the range northward, looking for a corridor to the other side. Judith had told him to keep searching. "Just try," was how she put it. He had and was now ready to give up.

Standing on a ridge, looking at the impenetrable wall of stone, he felt a breeze on his face. It didn't register at first. A backbreeze from the face of the cliff? He moved down the parapet, sensing a discovery.

Tucked in the granite face at an impossible angle was a path, an alley snaking through the great shield. Picking his way through the tight opening, he was glad to be moving forward. He looked back to gauge his distance. Two creatures faced him, spears ready to fly. Two more blocked the front. These small, fierce-looking beasts looked like the Rondthalers Judith had described. He had thought he was out of their territory. They took him to their camp on the far side of the mountains. At least they were going his way.

"What are you going to do with me?" asked the traveler.

"Du with yu, du with yu. Whi, hav fun, of cors," said the leader, a blunt, white-bearded beast.

"What do you mean? Please explain."

"Certinle," said the creature, "yu r our prissnr til yu can solv our ridl. Each da we wil ask yu tu spel a werd. If yu du not, yu wil b our slav as long as yu r here."

Each day a Rondthaler came to his hut and asked him to spell a word. He could only spell the words the way he had learned. He hadn't thought much about spelling; it hadn't been important till now.

"H-O-R-S-E"

Rong.

"G-H-O-S-T"

Rong.

"T-I-C-K"

Rong.

Day after day, the same exercise with the same results. The traveler despaired he would ever be free. He dug into his sack and pulled out the books Judith had given him on her last visit. Several concerned spelling. He read. No connections at first. The more he read, the more references he saw to simplified or phonetic spelling. This might be it! He would test his theory the next morning.

The tribesman arrived at the hut, ready to stump him again. "The werd for tuda is pepol," he said.

The traveler tensed, ready for the experiment.

"P-E-P-O-L," the traveler spelled.

The Rondthaler shrieked and ran out the door. Soon the headman appeared in the doorway. He was angry.

"I have your word of honor. I'm to be released," said the traveler. "But first, let me ask you a spelling."

The creature nodded in defeat.

In his reading, in his desperation to crack the code, the traveler had discovered that spelling told more than the letter makeup of the word. He was anxious to show how Rondthaler spelling would destroy that.

"How would you spell ineffectual?" asked the traveler.

The Rondthaler didn't hesitate. Slowly the letters were formed: "N-E-F-E-K-T-U-L."

"That's not the way we spell it," said the traveler, who then gave his spelling of the word. "You see, your system allows you to deal only with the sounds. My spelling tells me there's a root word— effect, an ending—ual, and a prefix—in. All of them have a specific meaning. My spelling is loaded with information; yours isn't.

With that, the traveler left the village, knowing that his telling hadn't changed the Rondthaler, but more prepared to answer those who advocate spelling reform.

The final leg of the journey took the traveler down from the mountains to the sea. A pebbly shingle connected this land mass with another. There were signs of those who had gone before. A cluster of shacks loomed ahead. He started across the beach, his quest entering a new phase.

A figure tracked him. He had been conscious of a presence many times during his journey. Could it be Judith? Why did she always come from behind? His pace quickened, unsure of the intentions of his pursuer. He hadn't seen Judith since last Tuesday, but he suspected, from the day he had found the brooch at the snake pit, that she was always near.

A belligerent voice intruded on his thoughts.

"Don't take another step!"

The voice came from a giant standing in his path, legs apart, arms folded at his chest.

"I am looking for the Key," said the traveler, growing tired of these challenges. "Please let me pass."

"You must prove yourself worthy to travel this path. You must defeat me in hand-to-hand combat, and only then m⁻ ⁻ you continue your quest."

"Who are you, and why do you interrupt my travels?"

"They call me The Great Conference," said the giant, holding his position on the trail. "There is no other way to the Key. You must confront me."

The traveler leaped, catching the giant offguard. They stumbled to the ground. The two twisted and rolled on the shingle, the sound of the pounding waves underscoring their battle.

The initial advantage was soon lost, and the giant pinned him easily. The traveler got to his feet and retreated, hoping to recoup.

The next day, he was back again. The struggle was brief. He felt that the Great Conference was playing with him. Again, the traveler retreated in defeat.

He had no strategy. This was a new enemy, a strong enemy, an enemy who easily thwarted his best efforts. He sat on the beach, dejected. A shadow darkened the white pebbles. He didn't have to look up, he knew it was Judith. She had seen his struggle.

"The Great Conference is not as big as you make him," she explained. "Go at him as you would an ordinary problem. Use some ingenuity. Think of another kind of confrontation. It doesn't have to be on his terms, you know."

He gave it some thought and went back for another try. The Great Conference took a combat stance. The traveler ignored it. Instead, he sat near the giant, unwilling to engage.

"That was a terrific hold you pinned me with yesterday," said the traveler. "Would you show me how you did it?"

The giant's arms went slack and dropped to his side.

"You have great strength. How do you use it? Is it wasted guarding this road, or do you do other things?

No one had spoken to the giant this way before. He was disarmed. He sat on the beach near the traveler. Already he looked smaller. He didn't feel like fighting anymore—he was interested in the traveler's questions.

For the next hour, the two men shared their knowledge of combat. The giant was adept at wrestling and demonstrated his moves. The traveler tried them. Some worked, others required more skill and strength than he possessed at the moment. As the sharing drew to a close, the two shook hands. The traveler continued his journey.

The trail led to a town. It marked a point in his passage, but was it an ending? Somehow, he felt this quest was self-renewing.

Sitting in a cantina, the traveler reviewed his experience. He had stepped in the wrong places, assumed certain truths, and had been guilty of narrow thinking, but with support, he had moved forward. He had known for some time there was no Key—the Quest was the thing.

Around the corner, in the same bar, sitting with a faceless monk, a droid, a grey-bearded Rondthaler, and a giant, was a leather-clad guide wearing a kite brooch.

Although we have cited few references, we did read extensively. We began the "Writing and Computers" class with a list of research articles and book chapters that I prepared for the class. These readings covered a broad range of conflicting views about writing and writing instruction. Before long, the teachers were bringing books and articles they thought interesting and relevant to share with the rest of us. Our reading helped us become members of the wider interpretive community.

The bibliography that follows is not intended to be exhaustive. It lists the selections we read as a group and includes recent books and articles about literacy instruction and change that the teachers and I found helpful for extending our discussion and developing a reflective stance.

BOOKS

Atwell, Nancie. 1987. *In the Middle.* Portsmouth, NH: Boynton/Cook.

Barnes, Douglas. 1976. *From Communication to Curriculum.* Portsmouth, NH: Boynton/Cook.

Bean, W. and C. Bouffler. 1987. *Spell by Writing.* Portsmouth, NH: Heinemann.

Bissex, Glenda L., and Richard H. Bullock, eds. 1987. *Seeing for Ourselves: Case-Study Research by Teachers of Writing.* Portsmouth, NH: Heinemann.

Calkins, Lucy. 1983. *Lessons from a Child.* Portsmouth, NH: Heinemann.

———. 1986. *The Art of Teaching Writing.* Portsmouth, NH: Heinemann.

Cambourne, B., and J. Turbill. 1987. *Coping with Chaos.* Portsmouth, NH: Heinemann.

DeFord, Diane, ed. 1980. *Learning to Write: An Expression of Language (Theory into Practice)*. Columbus, OH: College of Education.

Fulwiler, Toby. 1987. *Teaching With Writing*. Portsmouth, NH: Boynton/Cook.

Gamberg, R., W. Kwak, M. Hutchings, J. Altheim, and G. Edwards. 1988. *Learning and Loving It: Theme Studies in the Classroom*. Portsmouth, NH: Heinemann.

Gentry, Richard J. 1987. *Spel . . . Is a Four-Letter Word*. Portsmouth, NH: Heinemann.

Goodman, Kenneth. 1986. *What's Whole in Whole Language?* Portsmouth, NH: Heinemann.

Goodman, Kenneth S., Yetta M. Goodman, and Wendy J. Hood. 1989. *The Whole Language Evaluation Book*. Portsmouth, NH: Heinemann.

Goswami, Dixie, and Peter Stillman. 1987. *Reclaiming the Classroom: Teacher Research as an Agency for Change*. Portsmouth, NH: Boynton/Cook.

Graves, Donald H. 1983. *Writing: Teachers and Children at Work*. Portsmouth, NH: Heinemann.

———. 1984. *A Researcher Learns to Write*. Portsmouth, NH: Heinemann.

Hanna, Paul R., Richard E. Hodges, and Jean S. Hanna. 1971. *Spelling: Structure and Strategies*. Boston: Houghton Mifflin.

Harste, Jerome C., Kathy G. Short, and Carolyn Burke. 1988. *Creating Classrooms for Authors*. Portsmouth, NH: Heinemann.

Mayher, John S., Nancy Lester, and Gordon Pradl. 1983. *Learning to Write/Writing to Learn*. Portsmouth, NH: Boynton/Cook.

Murray, Donald. 1982. *Learning by Teaching*. Portsmouth, NH: Boynton/Cook.

———. 1984. *Write to Learn*. New York: Holt, Rinehart and Winston.

Newkirk, Thomas, and Nancie Atwell. 1982. *Understanding Writing*. Portsmouth, NH: Heinemann.

Newman, Judith M. 1984. *The Craft of Children's Writing*. Portsmouth, NH: Heinemann.

———. 1985. *Whole Language: Theory in Use*. Portsmouth, NH: Heinemann.

North, Stephen M. 1987. *The Making of Knowledge in Composition*. Portsmouth, NH: Boynton/Cook.

Papert, Seymour. 1980. *Mindstorms: Children, Computers, and Powerful Ideas*. New York: Basic Books.

Perl, Sondra, and Nancy Wilson. 1986. *Through Teachers' Eyes*. Portsmouth, NH: Heinemann.

Rhodes, Lynn K., and Curt Dudley-Marling. 1988. *Readers and Writers with a Difference*. Portsmouth, NH: Heinemann.

Romano, Tom. 1987. *Clearing the Way*. Portsmouth, NH: Heinemann.

Shanklin, Nancy L. 1982. *Relating Reading and Writing: Developing a Transactional Theory of the Writing Process*. Monographs in Teaching and Learning #5, School of Education, Indiana University.

Smith, Frank. 1982. *Writing and the Writer.* New York: Holt, Rinehart and Winston.

————. 1983. *Essays into Literacy.* Portsmouth, NH: Heinemann.

————. 1988. *Joining the Literacy Club.* Portsmouth, NH: Heinemann.

Wells, Gordon. 1986. *The Meaning Makers: Children Learning Language and Using Language to Learn.* Portsmouth, NH: Heinemann.

van Manen, Max. 1986. *The Tone of Teaching.* Toronto: Scholastic.

ARTICLES

Bean, John C. 1983. Computerized word-processing as an aid to revision. *College Composition and Communication,* 34: 146–148.

Bereiter, Carl. 1980. Development in writing. In *Cognitive Processes in Writing,* ed. L. W. Gregg and E. R. Steinberg, 73–96. Hillsdale, NJ: Lawrence Erlbaum Associates.

Bingham, Anne. 1982. Using writing folders to document student progress. In *Understanding Writing,* ed. T. Newkirk & N. Atwell, Portsmouth, N.H: Heinemann.

Blackburn, Ellen. 1984. Common ground: Developing relationships between reading and writing. *Language Arts,* 61: 367–375.

Boomer, Garth. 1984. Literacy, power and the community. *Language Arts,* 61(6): 575–584.

Boutwell, Marilyn A. 1983. Reading and writing process: A reciprocal agreement. *Language Arts,* 60: 723–730.

Britton, James. 1978. The composing process and the functions of writing. In *Research on Composing,* ed. C. Cooper and L. Odell, 13–28. Urbana, IL: NCTE.

Bruce, Bertram, Sarah Michaels, and Karen Watson-Gegeo. 1985. How computers can change the writing process. *Language Arts,* 62: 143–149.

Carnicelli, Thomas A. 1980. The writing conference: A one-to-one conversation. In *Eight Approaches to Teaching Composition,* ed. T. R. Donovan and B. W. McClelland, 101–131. Urbana, IL: NCTE.

Church, Susan. 1985. Blossoming in the writing community. *Language Arts,* 62: 175–179.

Coe, Rick. 1987. An apology for form: or, Who took the form out of the process? *College English,* 49(1): 13–28.

Collins, Alan, and Dedre Gentner. 1980. A framework for a cognitive theory of writing. In *Cognitive Processes in Writing,* ed. L. W. Gregg and E. R. Steinberg, 51–772. Hillsdale, NJ: Lawrence Erlbaum Associates.

Cooper, Charles R. 1977. Holistic evaluation of writing. In *Evaluating Writing: Describing, Measuring, Judging,* ed. C. R. Cooper and Lee Odell, 3–32. Urbana, IL: NCTE.

Daiute, Colette A. 1983. The computer as stylus and audience. *College Composition and Communication.* 34: 134–145.

Dickson, W. Patrick, and Mary A. Vereen. 1983. Two students at one microcomputer. *Theory into Practice.* 22: 296–300.

Edelsky, Carole. 1984. The content of language arts software: A criticism. *Computers, Reading and Language Arts*, (Spring): 8–11.

Edelsky, Carole, Kelly Draper, and Karen Smith. 1983. Hookin' 'em in at the start of school in a "Whole Language" classroom. *Anthropology and Education Quarterly*, 14: 257–281.

Edelsky, Carole, and Karen Smith. 1984. Is that writing—or are those marks just a figment of your curriculum? *Language Arts*, 61: 24–32.

Edwards, Joyce. 1985. Evaluating children's writing: Asking why as well as how. *Elements*, 16: 2–6.

Elbow, Peter 1987. Closing my eyes as I speak: An argument for ignoring audience. *College English*, 49(1): 50–69.

Flower, Linda S., and John R. Hayes. 1980. The dynamics of composing: Making plans and juggling constraints. In *Cognitive Processes in Writing*, ed. L. W. Gregg and E. R. Steinberg, 31–50. Hillsdale, NJ: Lawrence Erlbaum Associates.

Harste, Jerome C., Virginia A. Woodward, and Carolyn L. Burke. 1984. Examining our assumptions: A transactional view of literacy and learning. *Research in the Teaching of English*, 18(1): 84–108.

Healy, Mary K. 1982. Using student writing response groups in the classroom. In *Teaching Writing*, ed. Gerald Camp, 266–291. Portsmouth, NH: Boynton/Cook.

Hunt, Russell A. 1987. "Could you put in lots of holes?" Modes of response to writing. *Language Arts*, 64(2): 229–232.

———. 1989. A boy named Shawn, A horse named Hans: Responding to writing by the Herr von Osten method. *Responding to Student Writing: Models, Methods and Curricular Change*, ed. C. Anson, pp. 80–100. Urbana, IL: NCTE.

Kamler, Barbara. 1980. One child, one teacher, one classroom: The story of one piece of writing. *Language Arts*, 57: 680–693.

Levin, James, A., and Marcia J. Boruta. 1983. Writing with computers in classrooms: "You get exactly the right amount of space!" *Theory into Practice*, 22: 291–295.

Mayher, John S. 1985. Mental models of the composing process. Unpublished manuscript.

Mikkelsen, Nina. 1984. Teacher as partner in the writing process. *Language Arts*, 61: 704–711.

Murray, Donald. 1980. Writing as a process: How writing finds its own meaning. In *Eight Approaches to Teaching Composition*, ed. T. R. Donovan and B. W. McClelland, 3–20. Urbana, IL: NCTE.

Newkirk, Thomas. 1984. Archimedes' dream. *Language Arts*, 61: 341–350.

Newman, Judith. 1984. Language learning and computers. *Language Arts*, 61: 494–497.

———. 1985. Are students really learning what we want them to? *Reading—Canada—Lecture*, 3(2): 93–100.

———. 1987. Learning to teach by uncovering our assumptions. *Language Arts*, 64(7): 727–737.

———. 1988. Sharing journals: Conversational mirrors for seeing ourselves as learners, writers, and teachers. *English Education,* 20(3): 134–156.

Perl, Sondra. 1983. Understanding composing. In *The Writer's Mind: Writing as a Mode of Thinking,* ed. J. N. Hayes, 43–51. Urbana, IL: NCTE.

Rosenblatt, Louise. 1985. Viewpoints: Transaction versus interaction— A terminological rescue operation. *Research in the Teaching of English,* 19: 96–107.

Serebrin, Wayne. 1986. A writer and an author collaborate. *Language Arts,* 63: 281–283.

Shynal, Brenda. 1984. To learn or not to learn: Two demonstrations of teaching. *Highway One,* 7(3): 35–40.

Smith, Frank. 1983. Reading like a writer. *Language Arts,* 60: 558–567.

Strickland, James. 1987. Why we think grammar instruction works: Exposing the implicit model. *CSSEDC Quarterly,* 9(1): 6–7.

Woodruff, Earl. 1983. Computers and the composing process: An examination of computer-writer interaction. *ECOO Newsletter,* 4: 41–45.